From Welcome
to Windhoek:
A Judge's Journey

Rich Leonard

For Sarah,
Rich Leonard

LM Press
1001 Winstead Drive, Suite 285
Cary, NC 27513

ISBN: 978-1-7341086-4-4

Foreword

—

During my thirty-five years of working on policy issues for the Federal Judiciary, I've had the privilege of knowing many of the Nation's most preeminent judges and court officers. Among this group, Rich Leonard is legendary. This entertaining memoir shows why. The combination of great legal ability, administrative and technical know-how, and a larger-than-life personality made Rich one of the fathers of modern judicial case administration. The stories and insights he describes, whether in North Carolina, Washington, or Africa, convey the story of a man deeply committed to the delivery of justice. The world is a better place because of that commitment.

— Mark Miskovsky, Chief, Court Policy Staff,
Administrative Office of the United States Courts

What Others are Saying

—

Rich Leonard tells a story, his story, of a life's journey from Sunday family dinners on the farm in Davie County to ground-breaking international legal cooperative endeavors in Africa in a laid back and comfortable style. A life so full it is hard to imagine that one person could have experienced such varied and significant life events. But having been his colleague on the federal bankruptcy bench, I know firsthand that Rich is one of the very few who could and did! This memoir highlights a life devoted to public service, and in particular, to ensuring the efficient and fair administration of justice in this country and around the world.

— Stephani Humrickhouse,
Judge (Retired), NC Eastern District Bankruptcy Court

One of the pleasures of spending time with Rich – and this book will reveal many – is that he's a great storyteller. He's also a first-class teacher. Reading *From Welcome to Windhoek* is like spending an evening in front of the fire with a fine drink hearing about the latest travels of a warm-hearted, thoroughly engaging friend – and realizing later how much you've learned along the way. Though I knew some of the stories he tells – stories about extraordinary people, about climbing mountains and shooting rapids, about facing down danger and managing adversity – I was charmed anew and awed by the intensity with which he embraces life, people, and his greatest cause, the well-being of one of democracy's most important institutions, the courts. Characteristically, he's generous to the many people he's worked with, open about his joys and disappointments, and self-effacing about his own enormous contributions to justice in the U.S. and Africa. I highly recommend spending a little time in his company through this funny, sweet, sometimes poignant book.

— Donna Stienstra,
Senior Researcher, Federal Judicial Center

I absolutely loved the book – I binged it in one sitting. Fantastic storytelling that had me laughing out loud at least a dozen different times. It was truly a joy to read.

— Alexandra Davis,
Davis Legal Media

Rich Leonard is a man of many talents, including master storyteller. Here he chronicles his efforts to establish a workable judiciary in many new democracies of Africa while recounting his life story. I had the good fortune being a judge—and from 1983 to 1990 Chief Judge of his court—and vividly remember many of them, though not in the fascinating detail this narrative provides. A good read.

— W. Earl Britt,
Judge, U.S. District Court, Eastern District of North Carolina

An engaging romp through courts and down legal alleys on several continents.

— Kiki Skagen Munshi,
Senior Foreign Service Officer (Retired)

Table of Contents

—

Part I – Zambia

Part II – Tanzania

Part III – Namibia

Part 1
Zambia

—

Clay lies still, but blood's a rover;
Breath's a ware that will not keep.
Up, lad: when the journey's over
There'll be time enough to sleep.

A.E. Housman,
A Shropshire Lad (1896)

Chapter 1

—

A Summons to Lusaka

"It always seems impossible until it's done."
— Nelson Mandela

I was sitting in my chambers in my small courthouse in Wilson, North Carolina, one spring afternoon in 1994 when my phone rang. The caller said he was from the U.S. State Department and asked if I would consider going to Zambia as a consultant.

I didn't hesitate.

"Sure. Where is Zambia?"

He explained the where, what, and why behind the request. The Zambian people had recently adopted a new constitution modeled in many ways after ours. They wanted some American judges to help set up their new structure.

We agreed to talk again the next day. I thought he might be a quack, or at least that nothing more would come of it. But just in case, I did some preliminary research that evening.

When he called back, I said, "You've got the wrong guy. I am a tall, blond, white Southerner with a considerable accent. Zambia is a 100 percent black African nation. I don't think I will be effective."

He disagreed. He said they had been looking for recommendations from a number of sources and that my name had come up repeatedly. The Zambians wanted a judge with administrative experience, and early in my career I was the Clerk of the local federal district court. He asked if I would participate in a transatlantic call the next day to discuss the project further.

This call did not go well. Or so I thought.

On the line from Zambia was the senior civil servant tasked with setting up the new court structure. She later came to be a great friend. She spoke beautiful British English with an African accent, but the quality of the call was poor. I understood about every third word. Even so, I responded as best I could to what I thought she was saying.

Afterward, I called my State Department handler.

"The call was a disaster. I'm sorry I embarrassed you."

"Quite the contrary," he responded. "You've got the job."

STARTING OFF WITH A BANG

A few days before I was to depart, my handler asked about my travel plans. I was surprised he didn't know. But one thing I would later learn through years of traveling abroad was that not every branch of the State Department is always in sync. I told him his travel office had me flying to London and then taking Air Zambia to the capital of Lusaka.

He exploded.

"Those idiots. You can't fly Air Zambia. The airline is in debt to creditors all over the world. Every time one of their two jets touches down, creditors try to seize it, and they just take off again."

As a federal bankruptcy judge, I appreciated the finer points of debt, attachment, and property seizure. So I asked to be re-booked. My new ticket took me through South Africa, safe from the grasping clutches of creditors, and I went to bed feeling relieved.

But on the morning of my departure, while listening to NPR in the shower, I received an even bigger jolt. I heard that the international arrival terminal at Jan Smut Airport in Johannes-burg – the very airport where I was landing the next day – had just been bombed. I called my handler and asked if this might put a kink in my plans. He assured me everything would be fine.

And though I had to transit through an open-air tent hastily constructed as a makeshift terminal beside the still-smoking ruins of the bombed building, he turned out to be right, and I passed through Johannesburg without incident.

When I arrived in Lusaka, I was surprised to find a formal delegation had been assembled to greet me. As a youthful looking 45-year-old, I quickly realized I did not match their image of an American judge. I watched in amusement as they approached every older white male in the immigration line and asked optimistically, "Judge Leonard?"

Soon I was the only one left.

"I think you might be looking for me," I said.

Surprised but gracious, they escorted me to my hotel.

And there I was – 7,700 miles from my North Carolina home and light years from all that was familiar – at the threshold of what would become three decades of African adventures. My journey had begun with an unexpected summons to an unfamiliar place. And like all good journeys, this one would shape the course of my life in ways I had never imagined.

Chapter 2

—

In the Footsteps of Dr. Livingstone

"I will go anywhere, provided it be forward."
— David Livingstone

Like all nations, Zambia is a product of its geography and its history. The landlocked country of seventeen million people lies at the crossroads of central, south and east Africa. The first human fossil on the continent was found there in 1921, with the discovery of the Broken Hill skull.

The first European visitor of record was the Scottish physician, missionary, and explorer David Livingstone, who arrived in 1851. When he laid eyes on the magnificent waterfalls of the Zambezi, he named them for his queen, Victoria.

During one trip there, I followed the final path of Dr. Livingstone.

I visited the spot in northern Zambia where he died, and where his heart was buried under a tree, and from where an expedition carried his body for 63 days and more than a thousand miles to the coast. I went to where his body was kept on Zanzibar awaiting passage to England. And later, while in London, I visited his burial site in Westminster Abbey.

As I stood beside his gravestone – with its Biblical inscription, "Other sheep I have, which are not of this fold; them also I must bring, and they shall hear my voice." – I found myself moved. I had been to some of the places where this great adventurer had been. I had walked where he had walked more than a century before. Now I was at his final resting place.

This, I would come to discover, was but one of many connections – often unlikely, always enriching – my journey would offer.

HISTORY AS PROLOGUE

In colonial times, Zambia was known as Northern Rhodesia. It was largely an agrarian society until huge copper deposits were discovered in 1928. Since then, the national economy has risen and fallen with the price of copper on the world market.

After considerable controversy, Northern Rhodesia became the independent nation of Zambia in 1964. As in the United States and throughout Africa, ultimate prosperity has turned on the ability of the first presidents (who, like in the United States, were their revolutionary leaders) to surrender power at the end of their terms. In nations such as South Africa, Botswana, and Namibia, where the first president gracefully turned over the office to a democratically-elected successor, the political situation has been relatively stable and the nation generally prosperous. In others, such as Zimbabwe and Zambia, where the first president held on against all odds, instability and stagnation were the result.

In Zambia, Kenneth Kaunda became President upon independence. He immediately established one-party rule, and was re-elected in 1973, 1978, 1983, and 1988. I saw first-hand the calamitous consequences that occur when a leader refuses to yield power. The disintegration of the economy, violent strikes, and riots over food prices finally led Kaunda to step aside in 1991.

During my time there, the union leader, Frederick Chiluba, was president. He faced a coup attempt in 1997 by forces loyal to Kaunda. The coup was put down quickly. I sat through a number of initial proceedings of the 84 alleged participants arrested. For-ty-four were sentenced to hang in 2003. And though the record is not completely clear, the death sentence of the coup leader was commuted, as presumably were the others.

MERGING THE OLD AND THE NEW

It was not as if Africa had no laws before the colonial powers arrived. In fact, each clan or ethnic group has its own sophisticat-ed set of rules for marriage, inheritance, and property ownership, among other issues. Cases are decided by the chief or village elders. Reconciliation is the goal.

How countries integrate these traditions – known as customary law – into their national legal systems is fascinating.

For example, I was puzzled to see estate cases in Zambia where nephews were the heirs of a deceased man, to the exclusion of his own children.

It was explained to me like this: "The property must stay in the bloodline of the family. A man cannot know for sure that the children of his wife are his, or that the children of his brothers are theirs. But he knows that he and his sisters are of the same mother, so their children are indisputably of the family blood. So, their male children take."

Blending customary law into the judiciary isn't all that difficult procedurally. The first judicial level is usually called Local Courts or Customary Courts. An appeal from a decision there goes to the local Subordinate Court, presided over by a magistrate, and from there to the High Court and the Supreme Court.

More difficult is reconciling the substantive law and customary law.

This is particularly true when it comes to women's rights. Most customary law is unfavorable to the rights of women. This is so even though virtually every national constitution prohibits discrimination on the basis of gender.

Countries handle this issue differently. Some, like Zambia and Zimbabwe, expressly except customary law from the non-discrimination provisions of their constitutions. So, for instance in Zambia, although the inheritance scheme described above is completely contrary to the national intestacy laws passed by Parliament, it survives under the constitutional exception. But in Kenya, Malawi, and Uganda, the constitutions require customary law to conform to the constitutional provisions on non-discrimination.

DAWN ON DAY ONE IN LUSAKA

My first day in Lusaka started with a meeting with the Chief Justice, Matthew Ngulube, an amiable and gregarious guy who would become a close friend. We met in his office. What caught my eye were the three telephones sitting on his desk. When one rang, he would pick up each in succession until he found the right one. This was because there were three distinct and disconnected phone systems, one built by the Japanese, one by the Scandinavians, and one by the Americans. One worked internationally, one within Zambia, and the other only locally.

I came to see this as a metaphor for all of Africa. Uncoordinated aid, which the Africans gratefully accepted, came from all quarters. The effects were often confusing and duplicative.

Once we knew each other better, Chief Justice Ngulube told me a story. Early in his term, he said, he handed down a judgment in an election case unfavorable to the government. Late that night, the President's private security detail showed up at his residence and asked him to accompany them to the State House.

He was ushered into President Kaunda's office. After a few minutes of pleasantries, the President expressed his unhappiness with the judgment and asked the Chief Justice to rescind it. The Justice replied, "Mr. President, we are a constitutional democracy and we each have our roles. I have performed mine, and I assume you will do likewise." As he got up to depart, he thought he had at best a 50/50 chance of being allowed to leave. He was.

Years later, I was heartsick to read that the Chief Justice was embroiled in scandal. A secret Swiss bank account had been discovered in his name. Although professing his innocence, he resigned in disgrace. Later, a commission of inquiry believed his story that he had absolutely no knowledge of the bank account, but that it had been set up by President Kaunda as leverage against issuing unpopular judgments. Although he never returned to the court, he continues today as a leading member of the Zambian legal community.

RUNNING WITH CHILDREN, BUT NOT MARINES

Back then I was a daily jogger. That first afternoon in Lusaka, I took off from my hotel for a run. The porter chased me down. "I say, My Lord, have you left something I can fetch for you, or do you just trot?" It took me awhile to get used to the custom in Zambia and other African countries formerly under British control of addressing judges as My Lord or My Lady. But I did enjoy those daily trots.

Most Africans who walk everywhere find the Western habit of running for pleasure amusing. The children were especially intrigued. Before long, a group of 10 to 15 would be waiting for me every afternoon outside the hotel. We ran together, and what fun those miles were.

On a later trip, I was training for a marathon and increased my distance. At the ambassador's suggestion, I went to Marine House to look for a running partner. In every country in which we have a diplomatic presence, a small barracks of Marines is also there to guard our diplomats. At first the Marines were eager to join me. That is, until they asked how far I was running.

"Around 15 miles," I said.

They considered this, then said, "This is a safe country. We're sure you will be fine."

In my early trips to Zambia, Lusaka was indeed a safe city. The embassy provided me with an official driver during the day, but in the evening, I was on my own. I quickly identified a favorite taxi driver and tipped him well, so he was always on the lookout for me. He was a colorful character with a cab to match. One interesting feature was the lack of a backseat; I would sit on a folding lawn chair where the seat once was.

Going to a restaurant was always an adventure, and the phrase "brown bag lunch" took on a whole new meaning. The Zambian currency, the kwacha, had so devalued that you needed a massive roll of bills to buy anything. The government's response was to print even more money but refuse to concede to inflation by printing larger denominations. When eating out, I would bring a paper bag full of currency that had to be run through a kwacha counter, because counting it by hand would have taken too long.

All these experiences – tracing the footsteps of Dr. Livingstone, trotting with children through the streets of Lusaka, riding in my lawn chair with a sack of money – were unforgettable milestones on a memorable journey.

Chapter 3

—

Men Talk, Women Work

"He who does not know one thing knows another."
— African proverb

The basic trial court in Zambia is the High Court, as in Great Britain. The High Court in Lusaka consisted of eight judges: five men and three women. The judge in charge, called the Allocation Judge, was Irene Mambalima. She became one of my favorite judicial colleagues.

With the stature of a traditional African woman, and often wearing a native head scarf, Judge Mambalima was easy to underestimate. But watching her pillory lawyers in the courtroom, I quickly saw she had put her legal training at the University of London to good use.

At our initial meeting, she shared her frustration at the lack of case management. She had no idea how many cases were in the court, how many were assigned to each judge, or the procedural posture of each. A better system was desperately needed.

This was music to my ears.

I like systems. I always have. One of my first tasks as a young clerk of a federal district court was to devise an elaborate case management system basically from scratch. In three years, my court rose from near the bottom in the country in case dispositions to the top.

Why not try something similar for the High Court in Lusaka?

And so we set to work. I drew a random sample of the caseload and charted each case along several parameters to learn what was actually happening. The results were startling. Hundreds of cases had languished for years with no attention and no action.

No monitoring. No accountability. No system.

I discussed the results with Judge Mambalima and her two female colleagues over tea one morning.

"Do you three realize that you're doing eighty percent of the work of the court?" They shrugged.

"This is Africa," said Judge Mambalima. "Men talk. Women work."

The O.J. Simpson Trial as Seen in Zambia

Being a judge in Zambia, as throughout Africa, was hard work. There were no court reporters or reliable recording systems, so the judge's handwritten notes comprised the only official record. Needless to say, court was laboriously slow as everyone waited for the judge to transcribe the proceedings.

Not only that, but a basic underlying presumption that we take for granted was not shared there. Generally, when a case in the U.S. begins it has priority until it ends; other matters are pushed back. Not so throughout Africa. There, a case not concluded at the end of the session is reset to continue at the next available slot on the judge's calendar, which could be weeks or months away.

I came across the file of a murder case that had been tried on twenty-seven different days spread out over three years. Obviously, this compounds the logistical difficulties for witnesses and prisoner transportation.

I think, in large part, the different approaches to court dockets is a function of our use of jury trials, which invariably proceed from start to finish, even when the length greatly exceeds the initial estimate and requires that other matters be continued.

But I realized Zambia was in no rush to embrace a jury system. I was there in 1995 during the O.J. Simpson trial. The local judges followed the case closely. When the jury returned a verdict of not guilty, they were shocked by what they deemed a travesty of justice. Any interest they might have had for jury trials quickly vanished.

Everyone in the (Jury) Pool

Administering a jury system is extremely complex, a fact that few people – including many in the profession – fully appreciate.

I became keenly aware of these complexities when I served as the Clerk of U.S. Court for the Eastern District of North Carolina. One of my many responsibilities was managing the federal jury pool. After each presidential election, I estimated how large a pool we would need for the next four years. Federal jurors are drawn from the state-registered voter rolls. The Eastern District comprises 44 counties, ranging from metropolitan Wake (with 1.1 million citizens) to tiny Tyrrell (4,000). I calculated the percentage of the jury pool that should be supplied by each county, and then I collected those names to begin the qualification process.

In the larger counties, the process was easy. I would give the election supervisor the protocol (for instance, draw every fifty-third name), and they would provide the list to us.

In the smaller counties, not so much. To compile the list, my deputy clerks had to fan out across rural eastern North Carolina to manually copy the names from the local records, then return to manually enter the names in our system.

There was another problem. Federal law exempts some groups from jury service, such as policemen and firemen. The local courts can create additional exemptions. The jury plan I inherited, which was not unusual for its day, exempted a wide variety of professional groups, such as doctors, lawyers and teachers.

I did not like this.

If my life or liberty were at stake, I would not want these people excluded from my jury. Neither did Earl Britt, when he became Chief Judge of the Eastern District. Growing up like I did in rural North Carolina, he disliked elitism in any form. So we amended our jury plan to remove all exemptions, except for those required by federal statute.

This sometimes led to high drama. I remember once a local doctor was summoned to jury service, but he ignored us. He did not request to be excused. Nor did he request a postponement. He simply did not show up.

Judge Britt was not pleased. Without hesitation, he summoned the marshal and issued this directive: "Go to the doctor's office and enter through his waiting room. Unless it appears someone is there really sick, take him into custody and bring him to my courtroom."

Shortly thereafter, the shackled doctor arrived at the courthouse. When the marshal announced his presence, Judge Britt replied,

"I'm busy with another case now. Put him in the holding cell until I have time to deal with him."

That story spread like wildfire. Afterwards, my job assembling jury pools became much easier.

As a court, we were enormously proud of our jury usage figures. To the average citizen, this means nothing. But to us, it was a big deal. Often our numbers were the best in the country. We had almost no "wasted jurors," or people brought in who are never used. That was partly because we designed a system where we had calendar call and heard motions for continuance and pleas on Monday but waited until Tuesday – when we knew which cases would proceed to trial – to bring in the jury panel.

But even the finest system can falter, and occasionally ours did.

I recall one Monday when a defendant in a bank robbery trial pled guilty, so we called each prospective juror and told them not to show up the next day. On Monday afternoon, however, the defendant had a change of heart and withdrew his guilty plea. Now we needed a jury panel after all – and we had only hours to assemble one.

I turned to my able jury administrator.

"What," I asked, "did you say when you called off the panel?"

She blanched.

"I told them the guy came to his senses and pled guilty."

Oh my. We had just contaminated the panel and could not use them.

"Okay team," I said, as I called in my senior staff. "We've got a long night ahead of us."

And so, like a giddy group of college students, we proceeded to work late into the night calling jurors from a new panel we had drawn. We worked the phones until we had found enough new jurors for the next morning. The judge never knew what had happened.

The next day, I bought equipment so we could record messages for jurors, thus eliminating personal contact.

Later, I became a judge with the U.S. Bankruptcy Court, where jury trials are rare. Once, a case on my docket was headed for a jury trial. A jury pool was assembled. But on the day the jury was to be selected, the lawyers came to my chambers and said they had settled.

"No," I said. "You have not."

I told them if I wasted a whole panel of jurors, the district court would never draw another one for me.

"We are picking a jury and you are making opening statements," I told them. "Feel free to talk to me at lunch about settlement."

THE ADVANTAGES OF TRIAL BY FIRE

I believe I was a successful court administrator largely because of how I trained and used my staff. I was only 29 when I became clerk of the federal court. The staff I inherited was experienced – most of them older than me – and capable. But they had a narrow view of their job. They saw their role as mostly limited to taking the filings, recording them on the docket sheets, and placing them in the correct file.

I made some changes. I changed the position of deputy clerk to case manager, and I began hiring women and men straight out of local colleges and universities. I trained them extensively in the rules of civil and criminal procedure and the local rules of our court. Then I gave each of them a stack of cases to oversee and manage.

At least six of that initial group made court administration their career. Some became senior federal court administrators across the country. All contributed greatly to the judicial process. Playing a small role in their professional development is one of my proudest accomplishments.

I was never afraid to throw my young clerks directly into the fray.

I recall one new employee, Jolie Skinner, who was assigned to the front counter on her third day of work. A senior member of the bar, George Ragsdale, walked up and demanded service. He wanted me to issue a writ of attachment for some airplanes in Kansas as security in a lawsuit he had just filed.

Jolie brought his papers to my office. I told her that what he requested was completely improper because our attachment statute did not apply outside of North Carolina.

Jolie marched back to the counter and told Ragsdale what I had told her. He blustered a bit. He said he'd never heard such nonsense. Why, he had been doing this his entire career.

Jolie – a full seventy-two hours on the job – did not flinch.

"Sir," she fired right back. "This has been the policy of our office the entire time I have been here."

Jolie retired thirty years later as the operations manager of the court.

Powerpoint? What Powerpoint?

Flush with my success in the states, I suggested to my Zambian friends that educating and empowering their registry staff could produce similar results.

My enthusiasm was met with skepticism, to put it mildly. Their hierarchical system placed little importance on staff training. Nonetheless – and perhaps to placate me – they organized the first national training conference for senior registry staff. I was invited to attend the two-week event as a "resource person."

I was unsure what being a "resource person" entailed. I was fairly sure of the "person" part. And being a systems guy, I knew all about resources. So I prepared enough materials for a session or two.

Meanwhile, I was being assured that the event was tightly organized and the agenda firmly nailed down.

Arriving in Lusaka the Sunday evening before the conference began, I asked to see said agenda. A program organizer handed it to me with great pride.

The schedule for the first day went like this:

- 9 a.m. Judge Leonard commences
- 10:30 a.m. Tea
- 11 a.m. Judge Leonard continues
- 1 p.m. Lunch
- 2:30 p.m. Judge Leonard resumes
- 4 p.m. Tea
- 4:30 p.m. Judge Leonard concludes.

At this point, I was mildly discomforted. I realized I would have to stretch my material to fill the whole day. My discomfort turned to horror when I flipped through the agenda and saw the first page replicated nine times: Judge Leonard, tea, more Judge Leonard, lunch, more Judge Leonard.

That was it. I was the program. Me and more me, with breaks for tea. For two whole weeks.

Keep in mind this was in the mid-1990s, before the internet. Email was primitive, with no possibility of attaching documents to a message. In other words, there was no way to send an SOS for help from friends back in the states.

Talk about putting one's skills at organization – not to mention distance running – to the test.

Never have I worked harder: each night into the early morning spent weaving materials out of whole cloth for the next day. I called on (and by "called" I mean begged) my many Zambian friends to do guest lectures. I canvassed the senior registrars for their areas of expertise and enlisted them as a rump faculty to teach the others. We did mini-Toastmasters sessions, with everyone making a three-minute speech on any topic to boost confidence.

Somehow – almost miraculously – we managed to pull it off. The program was a success. When it was over, I flew home, drained but eager to discover what future miracles lay in store on this excellent journey I found myself on.

Chapter 4

—

Polyester, Patents, and Black-Eyed Peas

*"Despite what appears impossible at present, we can,
with determination and perseverance, still achieve the
kind of America we dream of."*
— Lawyer, educator and civil rights leader
Julius L. Chambers

One thing that fascinated me about the judicial system in Africa was not that its laws and procedures were unlike ours. I expected that. More interesting was its sometimes divergent attitude towards courts and judges in general.

For instance, African judges were keenly interested in the quality and quantity of staffing provided to American judges. This was demonstrated by the national training conference I helped organize in Lusaka.

But they were completely perplexed by our use of law clerks. The idea of putting young lawyers fresh out of law school at the side of powerful judges struck my African colleagues as odd, to say the least. Making these novices the judge's only permissible advisors struck them as ludicrous.

"Why don't you actually get someone who knows something?" was a frequent question.

But while I was and remain a staunch defender of law clerks, I must confess my feelings on the matter are intensely personal.

When I left North Carolina for Yale Law School, I always planned to return to my home state. Little did I know how parochial it was. Upon graduating from Yale in 1976, I might have gained a J.D. but had apparently lost my N.C. bona fides. Back then, no North Carolina law firms even deigned to interview in New Haven. Similarly, my inquiries about judicial clerkships were usually rebuffed – albeit politely, and with much Southern charm – with the explanation that the judge only hired graduates from North Carolina law schools.

Talk about keeping things in the family.

Imagine my surprise, then, to get a call from the office of Chief Justice Susie Sharp of the North Carolina Supreme Court, responding to my application for a clerkship and inviting me for an interview.

Chief Justice Sharp was a figure of legend. In 1949, she made history as the first woman in North Carolina appointed to the state Superior Court. She later made more history as the first woman in the country elected as a state Supreme Court Chief Justice.

My first challenge was simply getting from Connecticut to the Carolinas for the interview.

I lived modestly during my law school years. My diet largely subsisted of beans and rice received in exchange for volunteering at the nearby Hispanic co-op. To prepare for my trip to North Carolina, I began saving up toll money and hoping our ten-year-old Volkswagen Beetle would make it there and back.

In Raleigh, I was ushered into Chief Justice Sharp's chambers. We had a delightful chat – for about 15 minutes. Then she looked down at my file, and her demeanor changed completely.

"Wait," she asked in horror. "Are you in law school at Yale?"

I confessed I was.

She continued, her voice cold: "I misread your file. I thought you went to Yale for your undergraduate studies and had the good sense to come home for law school. I do not hire law clerks from Yale. Good day."

I slunk out. I was in Raleigh for about 30 minutes before climbing into my beleaguered Beetle and heading back to New Haven.

Interviews with two other judges in North Carolina went better.

I had a somewhat stilted chat in Raleigh with U. S. District Judge Frank Dupree. But I was awestruck in my interview with North Carolina Supreme Court Justice Jim Exum, who had just joined the Court. He was a hip, liberal motorcycle aficionado. We hit it off immediately.

I returned to New Haven hoping for an offer from one of them, but praying it would be Justice Exum.

My hopes were dashed when the deadline for their decision came and went, and I had heard nothing from either. Then one day, as I was leaving the law school to bike back to our apartment, a friend yelled at me.

"There's a note on the bulletin board for you," he said. "You need to call some North Carolina judge."

I raced back inside, fingers crossed it was Exum who had called. But no. It was Dupree.

Even so, I hurried to the nearest pay phone and made the call. After some pleasantries, Judge Dupree offered me a two-year clerkship in his chambers starting in September. The protocol is to accept on the spot, and I did. I biked home, relieved to have landed a job back home in North Carolina, but disappointed it was not the one I really wanted.

What should be waiting for me in the mailbox back home but a letter from Justice Exum. He also offered me a clerkship, but of course I was unavailable, having just accepted the offer from Judge Dupree. But such is the way of all journeys, full of twists and coincidences that turn out to be not coincidental at all.

First Impressions Don't Always Last

Another thing I've learned along the way: It's easy to misread a person.

In our first meeting, Judge Dupree struck me as gruff and taciturn, a conservative Republican with whom I would likely disagree on most things. But over time we developed a relationship as affectionate as father and son. He became my mentor and cheerleader for the rest of his days. My youngest son's middle name is Franklin, in his honor.

In the beginning, things were a bit shaky.

In 1976, I showed up in Judge Dupree's chambers a few days before I was actually supposed to start work. I wanted to get the lay of the land. Turned out one of his clerks had the flu and the other had just had a baby, and I was pressed into service.

"Well," said Judge Dupree. "Looks like you'll just have to be my clerk a bit early."

I had no idea what that meant. To my dismay, one requirement was to formally open the proceedings with the long "court in session" chant, which he preferred. Here I was just hours into my new job and already throwing out the ceremonial first pitch to start the game.

Helpfully, Judge Dupree wrote the chant out on an index card. Unhelpfully, he told me I could not carry the card into the court-room and read it. I was to memorize it, and quickly. Thinking fast, I transposed the chant onto the palm of my hand, in per-manent ink, and hoped the audience in that first session did not notice my frequent downward glances.

Somehow, I got through it.

Lessons From a Civil Rights Legend

My clerkship with Judge Dupree turned out to be quite different than expected. All of my friends from Yale had taken clerkships with federal judges in New York, Los Angeles, and Washington. There I assumed they would be in the midst of crucial cases making national headlines. On the other hand, I was returning to eastern North Carolina to watch trials of car wrecks and bank robberies.

But that was not to be.

The proceedings on my first day as a clerk were motions on remand from the U.S. Supreme Court in *Moody v. Albemarle Paper Co.* The case, brought by workers at a Roanoke Rapids paper mill against their employer, was one of the first pivotal opinions interpreting Title VII, the 1965 statute prohibiting employment discrimination.

Representing the plaintiffs was legendary civil rights attorney Julius Chambers. He sat alone at the plaintiffs' table with only a blank legal pad before him. Over at the defendants' table sat Whiteford Blakeney, the Dean of the North Carolina defense bar, surrounded by a small army of junior partners, associates, and paralegals. A mountain of paperwork containing the entire voluminous record of the case was piled before them.

Behind Blakeney sat the management of the paper company. All of them wore navy suits. Behind Chambers sat the workers at the paper mill. All were neatly attired in blue work overalls.

The contrast could not have been greater.

I was stunned by the brilliance of Julius Chambers. He won the day, answering all of Judge Dupree's questions with precision and ease, citing the record by page number without references in front of him. This was a master class in trial advocacy.

I left work that afternoon exhilarated. I had somehow stumbled into a position where significant issues were debated with skillful advocacy and intellectual rigor. I felt like the luckiest law clerk in the world.

That feeling stayed with me for the two years I was with Judge Dupree.

LARGEST PATENT CASE IN THE COUNTRY

During my tenure as Judge Dupree's law clerk, the largest patent and antitrust case in the country at the time was pending in South Carolina. This was a lawsuit by virtually every textile manufacturer in the country against Deering Milliken, challenging the patents on the machines from which polyester was spun.

At issue was all of the polyester ever made from these machines.

Every South Carolina federal judge, either because of their friendship with Roger Milliken or ownership of stock in his company, recused themselves. Consequently, the Chief Judge of the Fourth Circuit assigned the case to Judge Dupree for trial.

And so Judge Dupree packed up his court apparatus, including myself and his other law clerk, and headed down to South Carolina, where we commandeered the small, vacant federal courthouse in Rock Hill. My co-clerk and I alternated weeks traveling there with him for the trial.

The case involved dozens of top-tier lawyers and numerous expert witnesses, and it was hopelessly complex. I went to bed every night with drawings of textile machines, trying to understand how they worked.

Judge Dupree quickly tired of hotel life in Rock Hill and rented a modest two-bedroom apartment for us. Not afraid to pinch a penny, he enjoyed coming into town for grocery shopping every Sunday afternoon. On the weeks I accompanied him, he would try to spend less than he and the co-clerk had the previous week.

Suffice it to say, we ate simply.

The lengthy Deering Milliken trial finally reached closing arguments. Simon Rifkind – the highest paid civil attorney in the country – was making his pitch.

Judge Dupree looked over and got my attention. He held up his hand for Rifkind to pause and motioned for me to come to the bench.

I leaned my ear close as he whispered, "You better run back home. I don't think I put enough water in the crock pot with those black-eyed peas. Better go check them before we burn the place down."

I raced out of the courtroom, drove his enormous Carolina-blue Mercury back to the apartment, and added water. Disaster averted, I stepped back into the courtroom, where closing arguments were still in progress, and flashed a big OK sign.

To this day, lawyers ask me what that was all about. They're convinced Judge Dupree had sent me running off to research a legal point that was pivotal in his decision to award the plaintiffs more than $40 million in damages. Little did they know I was making sure the black-eyed peas were not burning.

A QUESTION OF ETHICS

Like I said, I am a fan of law clerks, and not just because of my positive experience as one. I believe the institution of law clerks is one of the bedrocks of American justice. Partly this is because judicial clerkships are laboratories for teaching – and modeling – professional ethics.

I recall once in Raleigh we were catching up on our criminal docket, and a young law student home on his Christmas break wandered into our library. He said he was watching a bank robbery trial Judge Larkins was conducting in the other courtroom. We chatted politely as he browsed through the federal criminal code. Later, my co-clerk and I were surprised when one of Judge Larkin's clerks said they had a law student on the jury. Then when the jurors retired in a simple case, questions were sent out to Judge Larkins that could only be posed by a first-year law student – perhaps one who had just been browsing in the courthouse law library and chatting with clerks of another judge.

When Judge Dupree mentioned Judge Larkins' exasperation at the questions, I innocently said, "That's because he has a law student on his jury."

Judge Dupree stopped in his tracks.

"How do you know that?"

We sheepishly confessed the law student-slash-juror had been in the library talking to us, but emphasized it was harmless.

Judge Dupree was having none of it.

"A juror in violation of his solemn oath was in my library talking to my law clerks about a case? Go right now and tell Judge Larkins."

We begged him to reconsider, but in the end, my clerk mate and I made our way down the hall, heads hanging. First, Judge Larkins interrogated us. Then, he brought in the lawyers to hear our story. Finally, we were examined under oath in the courtroom on the record.

Yes, there is an opinion on appeal. It held the jury tampering by the law clerks was harmless error. And I am eternally grateful the opinion did not mention our names.

Needless to say, I did not share that anecdote with my African colleagues as I tried to sell them on the value of judicial law clerks.

Chapter 5

—

My Hardest Walk ... And Hardest Talk

"Almost halfway."
— The consistent response of our Swahili-speaking
Kilimanjaro guide, John Mtui, when asked
how much further.

When I think of Zambia, I think of family. Many of the people I met there became like family to me. Many of my fondest memories stem from the time I spent there with each of my older sons, on very different trips.

My eldest son, Matt, was a serious, disciplined, and accomplished student. Working as an intern in the American Embassy in Lusaka was his cup of tea.

We finished off his time there with a bang, climbing Mount Kilimanjaro.

The trip itself had a back story involving one of my closest friends, John Edwards, former U.S. Senator and vice-presidential candidate.

John and I met as law clerks for Judge Dupree, our desks facing each other in an open library. John is from Robbins, N.C., and

I am from Welcome, N.C. No one in either of our blue-collar families had ever gone to college. We each possessed exactly two suits and three dress shirts. In other words, we were more like brothers than co-clerks.

CLIMBING MOUNT RAINIER

Within a week, we started running together, which we continued for about twenty years until he left for Washington, D.C. During our long runs we had hours and hours of conversation. One frequent topic was our shared phobia of heights. We decided the only cure was to climb a tall mountain, so we reserved spots to summit Mount Rainier and flew to Washington.

During the mandatory training day before the climb, John fell and pulled a groin muscle. I offered to just cancel and go home, but he wouldn't hear of it.

The Mount Rainier climb was horrendous. A blizzard hit at about 3:00 in the morning, and our guides literally got in a fist fight over whether we were safer to climb up out of the storm or go down. We went up, and I still recall sitting on a ledge sucking on frozen raisins, the snow barreling down, wondering how this happened. But the decision was correct, and we safely made it to the top and back down.

John met me at the bottom and told me he already registered us to return the next summer — once a year was as frequent as was allowed. At that point, it was the last thing on earth I ever wanted to do again.

I agreed to do it.

Fast-forward to my son Matt joining me in Lusaka, and I had a new challenge to throw at John and his 16-year-old son, Wade.

"Why don't you fly over with Wade and meet us in Tanzania, and we'll do the Big Walk, as the locals call climbing Kilimanjaro?" John readily agreed, and I set about making the necessary arrangements. We wanted as private a climb as possible, which meant hiring a private guide and porters, and then heading up the more obscure back trail.

BOY WITH SICK FEET

The trip almost came unglued at several points. Wade's mother, Elizabeth, was so concerned about his conditioning she sent him to Outward Bound in the Rocky Mountains to train. He arrived with such blisters on his feet he could barely walk. Our terrific guide, John Mtui, called him "Boy with Sick Feet." The first day was rough going, but we figured out that if Wade and I traded hiking boots, my slightly larger ones wouldn't rub so badly.

The second day, my ever-polite son forgot the rules and took a slug of water from one of the porter's jugs. By nightfall, his intestinal system was trash, as diarrhea hit, and he was convulsively throwing up. I woke John in the middle of the night and said I was sure we had to go back down, but he and Wade should continue. But by morning, Matt said he was feeling better and refused to quit.

We had a couple of days of pleasant climbing. At about 17,000 feet, John and I turned to each other simultaneously and said, "My head is splitting."

The altitude sickness we feared had hit with a vengeance. The prescription diuretics gave me some relief, but not John. He got progressively worse. The night before we were to start for the summit, it was assumed that I would go up with the boys and he would rest in the tent. But when it was time to depart, I found John in his cold weather climbing clothes.

He was going with us.

He lasted about two hours, when his labored pace slowed us down so much that the boys were freezing. They were doing the trick they learned in Outward Bound to avoid frostbite by putting their bare feet on a buddy's stomach.

John and I sat on a rock, and I said, "What do you want here?"

"I want Wade to get to the top," he said.

"Then you've got to go back down and let us go up, or we won't make it at this pace," I said.

He saw the truth in this and reluctantly agreed.

TWICE TO THE KILIMANJARO SUMMIT

I climbed with the two boys through the night and saw the sun rise over the summit. It was the experience of a lifetime. About two hours into the climb down, we were stunned to see John with a single porter laboring up the mountain. He had not gone down at all; just waited on us to get out of sight.

I could tell he was spent. I told the boys to go back to base camp with our guide and wait for us. Then I took one end of John's walking stick, and his porter took the other. He held onto the middle and the three of us went back to the top.

He said, "You don't have to do this."

"I know. But if you think I'm going to leave you here to die on this mountain alone and go home and face Elizabeth, you really are hallucinating."

So, I reached the summit twice.

Luckily, altitude sickness abates quickly as you descend. By the next day, John and Matt (the better athletes of the four of us) were racing down the trails, and Wade and I were straining to keep up.

A Shining Light is Lost

I had known Wade since he was born, as our families regularly spent time together. But we got especially close on this trip. Matt and I had shared a small hotel room in Lusaka for a couple of weeks, and Wade and John had been traveling for several days. Each son was ready to spend time with the other dad. Wade got stronger and stronger as we climbed higher, and I remember his excitement when he reached the summit.

"I never thought I could do anything this hard in my life," exulted my close friend's son, who had become like a son to me as well.

Nine months later, tragedy struck.

Wade was killed in a freak afternoon car accident on the way to his family's beach house for Easter. It was the most devastating loss I have seen good friends suffer. I could not stop thinking of our time together on Mount Kilimanjaro and how close we had become on the climb. I was asked to deliver the eulogy at his funeral. It was the hardest speech I ever gave.

Chapter 6

—

Chopsticks

"Jump over a log but not over your neighbour's word."
— Zambian proverb

Some of my time in Africa involved being a father, and trying to be a good one.

My second son, Justin, joined me in Zambia the year after his brother Matt was there. It was a very different trip. To someone as outgoing and fearless as Justin, the idea of an internship at the embassy was cruel and unusual punishment.

Casting about for a better fit for Justin, one of our diplomats said a British archaeologist brought a group of English students each summer to dig at Mumbwa Caves in central Zambia, one of the ancient riverbanks where we may have morphed into homo sapiens. She said the professor probably would not object to an extra pair of hands.

I contacted him, and he readily agreed to take on Justin.

BIRTHDAY CAKE AND LUGGAGE TIES

Justin and I landed in Lusaka late one Sunday afternoon. Early Monday morning, a Land Rover filled with English students sped into the hotel parking lot. Without missing a beat, Justin grabbed his trunk and jumped in.

I knew my son and was not the least bit concerned when I did not hear from him for a while. But our ambassador felt otherwise. He kept quizzing me about whether I was checking on my son, and how he was doing. Finally, he decided we would go out to the dig over a weekend and see for ourselves.

We began making the arrangements. This, itself, was an ordeal. I was never able to actually speak with Justin. The students alternated days at the local hotel in Mumbwa, where they showered and used the phone. I left Justin a message that the ambassador and I would be visiting on Saturday. In turn, he left me a message to bring luggage ties, a birthday cake, colored pencils, a sketch pad, and chopsticks. These struck me as unusual requests. Then again, unusual requests from this particular son were commonplace. Off I scurried to comply.

I got the hotel chef to bake a birthday cake, found luggage ties at the American Embassy, and purchased colored pencils and a sketch pad at the hotel gift shop.

But my piece de resistance was the chopsticks. I persuaded the only Chinese restaurant in Lusaka (for a nominal sum) to part with a dozen pairs of ivory chopsticks. I carefully explained they were critical for the archaeological dig.

With my shopping list complete, I joined the ambassador's three-vehicle entourage – Marines Corps' vehicles front and back, with us in the middle – to race halfway across Zambia on a gorgeous day under the bluest sky ever.

At the dig, the professor was overjoyed at the honor of hosting the ambassador. We drank wine under the hot sun and feasted on the sumptuous lunch his cook prepared. I presented the gifts I had brought to my son and his colleagues, to the delight of all. Our dessert was the birthday cake for the English lass Justin had moved into his tent, and the sketch pad and colored pencils were also for her. The professor especially appreciated the luggage ties, as he had run through his supply.

I waited until the end for my dramatic conclusion. I handed each student a pair of ivory chopsticks. They all nodded appreciatively, but I noticed their quizzical expressions as they eyed the chopsticks.

As we packed to go, Justin gave me a hug and thanked us for coming. He said it had been a perfect day.

"But one thing, dad. What was that bit with the chopsticks?"

I looked confused.

"That's what your message said, son. Bring a birthday cake, sketch pad, colored pencils, luggage ties and chopsticks. I thought you needed them to pick up tiny artifacts."

He laughed.

"Chapstick, not chopsticks, Dad. It's 100 degrees out here and our lips are parched."

WATCH FOR CROCODILES

Although we weren't able to climb Kilimanjaro, we did end that trip with another spectacular adventure, this one involving whitewater.

Until the 1980s, the Zambezi River below Victoria Falls was thought to be unnavigable by any craft. But then huge and tough rafts were built, and it became the most dangerous and exhilarating white water raft trip in the world. You climb down stairs carved into the cliff beside Victoria Falls as the mist sprays you, climb into these enormous rafts the size of a small house, and fly over Class V rapid after Class V rapid.

When we capsized in the first rapid, the guide looked around and pointed to Justin and me.

"You two, switch places and take the front oars."

He told the smaller couple from Hong Kong who had taken the front seats to go to the back. As she was moving, the lady said, "I say, are there crocodiles in this river?"

"Yes," said the guide.

"I say, what should we do if we capsize again?" She was clearly alarmed.

"Don't swim for shore. They don't like the rapids."

He patted his sidearm to give us extra comfort.

THE BUNGEE JUMP OF DREAMS

Although my boys had very different trips, each suffered the same grave disappointment of not checking one particular item off their bucket lists – bungee jumping off the Zambezi River bridge.

The seed was planted when Matt accompanied me in Zambia, and we joined a couple of diplomats in a car ride to spend the weekend at Victoria Falls. The largest commercial bungee jump in the world is off the bridge over the Zambezi River connecting

Zambia and Zimbabwe at Victoria Falls.

Matt was hellbent on doing it. And my relationship with my jock sons was such that, if they did it, I had to also, or be forever shamed.

One day we tried to make it happen, but we ran out of time as we waited in line. We knew we had to leave at ten o'clock sharp in order to make it back to Lusaka before dark. There was no flexibility. The four-lane highway into Lusaka turned to red dirt a few miles out of town (apparently the Japanese foreign aid financing the road ran out before construction was finished) and we had to be on the road no later than ten. Unfortunately, as the hour approached, we were still about ten people back in line. Reluctantly for my son, and with a huge sigh of relief from me, we had to abandon our place in the bungee-jump line and head back to Lusaka.

This incident was later mischaracterized as a ploy by me to avoid bungee jumping. The next summer, Matt warned his brother Justin I might try a similar ruse. I assured them I would not.

On the day Justin and I had planned our jump, Justin woke us at dawn to get in line early. Unbeknownst to us, jump day happened to fall on the weekend of the famous Rugby World Cup, when the underdog South African Springboks upset the New Zealand All Blacks. It turned out New Zealanders ran the bungee operation. This was a crushing defeat for New Zealand.

When Justin and I got to the jump site, half asleep in early morning, a hastily printed sign read: "Due to a day of national mourning, bungee is closed."

Saved again.

RUNNING ON LION TIME

My time in Zambia fell into a comfortable rhythm: Weekdays were filled with intense activity, and weekends were for exploring. The largely unheralded but stunning national game parks in the Luangwa River valley in northern Zambia were my favorite. A short plane ride from Lusaka on a Friday afternoon, and you were whisked into a tropical world with only a few tourist camps on the banks of the Luangwa River interrupting the scenery.

I learned to appreciate small comforts.

One Friday, a guide told me, "We have just cleared three black mambas from your cabin and there are no more."

Good to know.

The weekend before, some guests drinking sundowners on the riverbank watched in horror as a native fisherman on the other bank got too close to the edge. A lunging crocodile grabbed him and pulled in. The guides ran for their rifles, but it was too late.

Every afternoon, we took off into the bush in a nightly hunt for elephants, giraffes, lions, cheetahs, leopards, buffalo, and every manner of what we came to call "deer-like things."

And, to illustrate the insanity of the long-distance runner, on one trip to Africa I was training for a marathon and needed to get some long runs in. The guides initially said I should not leave the compound under any circumstances. I persisted, and they caucused and relented.

It sounds like lunacy now, but if you've trained for a marathon, you know how compulsive one can become.

"We believe if you go precisely at noon and return by half past one," my guides instructed, "and run just on this dirt path, you will likely be safe."

Impressed that African predators had such a keen sense of time, I took their advice and went for my training runs every day.

Chapter 7

—

Why You Not Treated Like a Big Man?

"The mouth puts the head in trouble."
— African proverb

One of the joys of my African work was I could occasionally carve out a role in a particular project to bring colleagues – either law clerks or court staff – to help. Computers were new to most judges in the 1990s, and certainly to African judges. Training was delicate. Although they had knowledgeable court staff, judges in that hierarchical system were hesitant to reveal ignorance to their subordinates. I didn't have much more luck working with them one on one, but it turned out my law clerks and court staff were the perfect individual tutors.

So I brought them to Africa with me.

On one trip with my career law clerk, Susan Hauser, and a supervisor in the Clerk's Office, Gayle McDowell, we went adventuring over a long Easter weekend. Sally Permar, a Duke student doing an internship there, joined us. She is now the imminent pediatric immunologist at Duke Medical School and appears regularly on NPR. Back then, she was just my regular running buddy.

Susan was my staff attorney at the district court, and I invited her to move with me to the bankruptcy court as my career law clerk. She stayed for the first half of my tenure there. A careful analyst and brilliant writer, she was a mainstay.

On one occasion, I was headed to Zambia during a semester I was also teaching the bankruptcy course at North Carolina Central University School of Law in nearby Durham. I told Susan she had to teach my class. Introverted and shy of the limelight, she was horrified at the prospect. I persisted. She prepared meticulously and substituted for me. It went well, so much so that she retooled her career and ended up a tenured law professor at that school. Recently, she was the first law professor to ever receive the annual system-wide award for excellence in teaching across the seventeen-campus University of North Carolina.

Susan, Gayle, Sally, and I booked a reservation in a remote fishing camp on the Zambezi River. At the wheel, we drove about eighty kilometers out the Great East Road — a two-lane road once paved but now mostly red dirt — then turned down another dirt path for thirty kilometers to hit a dead end at the Zambezi River, at the point where Zambia, Zimbabwe, and Mozambique touch. There, as scheduled, a motorboat appeared to take us about ten kilometers up the river to the camp.

We ran out of gas in sight of the camp and had to row the last hundred yards.

On a "walk-about" that afternoon, we stumbled upon a young bull elephant shot by a poacher and obviously in tremendous pain. Our concerned guides told us to step backward slowly. They raised their rifles to shoot, should he charge. We backed away without incident. The guides were immediately on their shortwave radios, and later that afternoon a plane, carrying a veterinarian, landed on the river. He found and sedated the elephant, packed the wound, and shot him full of antibiotics, then was gone as quickly as he came.

That night, after the women retired, I was in my usual spot matching drinks with the locals. On the other side of the river, we heard loud splashing.

"That is the lions entering the river. They will swim and come to the island and stop."

It happened as he predicted, but then the splashing started again, getting closer.

"Where are the lions now?" I said with trepidation.

"They are on our side of the river, in front of Susan's chalet."

Susan's chalet was a three-sided concrete structure open to the river on the fourth. Mosquito netting covered the opening.

"Should we be worried?"

I was.

"Oh, no. The rains have been plentiful this year and game is good. The lions have no interest in Susan."

We returned to our toddies.

GRITS AND DIPLOMACY

Because of my African experiences, I was frequently asked to host African judges and court officials when they visited the United States.

On his first visit, the Zambian Chief Justice, Matthew Ngulube, asked the State Department to invite me to D.C. to accompany him. I was delighted to do so, as it turns out the State Department has killer seats at Camden Yards. That Sunday, the Orioles were playing the Yankees. Trained since birth to hate the Yankees, I explained that the Orioles were our team.

Although Chief Justice Ngulube was a sportsman, baseball is a difficult game to explain to someone who has never seen it played. That a called third strike is an out and a towering fly ball caught in center field is an out, and they are the same thing, is not intuitively obvious. But he was a good student and cheered loudly when the Orioles went up 2-0.

I took a bathroom break in the eighth inning, and while I was gone the Yankees loaded the bases. When I returned, he grabbed my arm with a look of concern.

"Sit quickly," he said. "The enemy is threatening."

From Camden Yards, I was to transport Chief Justice Ngulube to Richmond to visit with Judge Robert Merhige. I knew Judge Merhige because he sat as a visiting judge in the Eastern District of North Carolina and we had overlapped in Zambia on my first trip there.

I realized as we traveled that the Chief Justice was barely picking at his food. Zambians eat very simply. Their staple is nshima, a dry porridge made of corn meal. You form it into balls, make an indentation with your thumb, and then use it as a base for other foods.

I pulled into a greasy spoon breakfast place on the way to Richmond and ordered a large bowl of plain grits. Chief Justice Ngulube wolfed down the bowl of grits, asked for another, and then another. He wrote down "grits" on a piece of paper so he would know what to order for the rest of his trip.

WHERE'S THE NICE CAR?

My African visitors were always enormously impressed with our courts, particularly with our physical facilities and our technology. But they consistently voiced two concerns.

"Why does your government not give you a nice car?" was one. African judges are used to the symbols of power, including expensive cars and drivers at government expense. They were astounded I had to buy my own on a judicial salary.

Even more concerning to them: "Why do they not treat you like a big man?"

My visitors were always surprised at the level of easy informality and warm camaraderie between my chambers and court staff and me. In their system, hierarchy is everything. Remember, judges are "My Lord" and "My Lady," and the style is autocratic.

This was brought home to me on one of my last trips to Zambia. Once we had developed some basic case management rules, we set about doing some simple automation. Our government bought enough computers for several young registry workers. They needed to be trained.

I was a Morehead Scholar at the University of North Carolina, and I knew they funded an international summer program for the scholars after their junior years. I also knew a young Morehead, Oliver Carter, who might be of help. I met "Ollie" when he was a junior in high school in Wilmington. His dad was a prominent lawyer who appeared frequently before me, but he was despairing of Ollie's hijinks.

"That boy is either going to win the Morehead or go to prison. Maybe both."

I suggested I could help by taking Ollie to dinner whenever I was in Wilmington for court. He avoided prison, and he did win the Morehead.

A Zambian Summer for a Morehead Scholar

Ollie jumped at the chance to spend a summer in Zambia, and he accompanied me to set up the training program for the young registry workers. Ollie lived in a storybook guest cottage behind one of our diplomatic residences, made close friendships with the young Zambians, and did a terrific job.

I suggested to the Chief High Court Judge, Irene Mambalima, that a word of encouragement to the young registry workers for their good work would be greatly appreciated. She thought it the oddest suggestion ever, but eventually agreed to it. She pushed back from her desk and said, "We will go now. Where is my registry?"

Chapter 8

—

The Youngest Court Clerk and the Jeffrey McDonald Trial

"The jury voted three times. On the first ballot, they were 7-5 for conviction; on the second 9-3; and on the third and final vote, they were unanimous."
— Jeffrey McDonald trial verdict, 1979

I did not set out to be the youngest U.S. District Court Clerk in the country, but that's what I became in 1979.

There was no master plan. After my time as a law clerk to Judge Dupree ended, I made the predictable move to enter private practice. I took a position with Senator Terry Sanford's law firm in downtown Raleigh.

About a year later, Judge Dupree called and invited me to drop by for a chat.

In his chambers, he told me he would become Chief Judge in a couple of weeks. Under federal law, the chief judgeship term for district and circuit courts is seven years, after which you must surrender the position to the next senior judge.

"My first official act will be to fire the Clerk of Court," he said.

Although appointments of court officials are made by a majority of the judges, Judge Dupree could do it unilaterally because the other two judgeships were vacant, and the senior judge who had been chief now had no vote.

"Interested in the job?" he asked me. "You were always messing around in administrative stuff that was none of your business when you were my law clerk, so you clearly like it."

Although it may appear from the outside that every court runs about the same, nothing is further from the truth. The Eastern District of North Carolina was in shambles. There was no system for doing anything. I knew I would be stepping into a quagmire.

Still, I was intrigued.

Judge Dupree continued, "Give me two or three years to get this place straight, then I'll make sure you go back to private practice without missing a beat."

I thought about it and signed on. It seemed a lot more fun than answering interrogatories in my windowless office at the firm.

I was 29 years old. The Administrative Office of the Courts told me they found no record of anyone so young assuming the position of U.S. District Court Clerk.

Some of my friends thought I had lost my mind to walk out of a top-tier firm and take a job that didn't require a law degree. My dad was particularly unimpressed, as the Clerk of the local court back home had formerly been a used car salesman.

But I knew otherwise. The benign label of "clerk" masks enormous authority, particularly if you have the backing of the judges. You hire and supervise a vast staff, oversee numerous federal courthouses, and run a financial enterprise of tens of millions of dollars.

THE GREEN BERET MURDER CASE

Plus, there was the opportunity to be part of the action on high-profile cases. I was originally supposed to start as District Court Clerk on a Monday morning in July. But Judge Dupree called and said he needed me to be sworn in on the Friday before. He was starting the Jeffrey McDonald murder trial on Monday morning and needed someone to manage all of the details.

Once again, I was fortunate to be in the right place at the right time. This was one of the most celebrated criminal cases of the past half-century. Jeffrey McDonald was a former Green Beret and emergency room doctor at Fort Bragg whose wife and two young daughters were brutally murdered in their apartment. Dr. McDonald claimed a group of chanting hippies broke in and did it. The grand jury thought otherwise and indicted him for murder.

Although the case had initially been assigned to Judge Dupree years earlier, it had bypassed me when I worked for him as a law clerk. It was pending at the time in the United States Court of Appeals for the Fourth Circuit, and then the Supreme Court, in review of Judge Dupree's order refusing to dismiss the indictment as a violation of the defendant's right to a speedy trial. The Fourth Circuit reversed Judge Dupree and ordered the indictment dismissed, but the Supreme Court reversed the Fourth Circuit and sent it back for trial.

Now the McDonald case was back in our court. This time, I was managing it.

I spent the weekend negotiating with national and local press about space and access, then setting the rules for the hundreds of spectators who wanted into the courtroom. All was in place and working smoothly.

Ironically, I had little time to actually watch the trial. I was swamped with the responsibilities of a new job I had abruptly inherited with no transition whatsoever. An initial shock came when I realized I was individually responsible for more than $40 million in the court registry.

Mismanagement was everywhere. Here's an example, involving processing of payments for misdemeanors: Federal courts have jurisdiction over all crimes committed on federal property within their geographical area. (That's why the McDonald case was in federal court, the crime having occurred at Fort Bragg.) Minor misdemeanors are handled by citations written by federal law enforcement officers. The originals were mailed to the local federal court, and if payment comes in the mail, it was matched to the citation and the case was closed. If payment was not received, the case went on a trial calendar. These are now all processed nationally.

During my first week, the young deputy clerk in charge of match-ing payments to citations brought me a briefcase stuffed with checks he could not match. Some dated back more than a year. I asked him why he never told my predecessor about this, and he visibly trembled and said, "He would have gotten so mad."

It took me weeks to sort it out.

Another deputy clerk in my Fayetteville divisional office told me she thought something suspicious was going on with finances. She suspected the retired Army colonel, her supervisor. Every Friday night for several weeks, she snuck the financial ledgers out of the office and met my financial deputy in the Hardee's parking lot in Angier. We'd spend the weekend in our Raleigh office trying to figure out his scheme – he had developed an elaborate method of writing fake receipts for fine payments at the counter, then pocketing some of the money – and on Sunday night they would reverse the transfers.

I summoned the suspect to Raleigh, told him I knew about his scheme, and showed him my evidence. I told him to give me his office keys and never return to the courthouse. As he dissolved into tears, I cautioned him not to say anything, as an FBI agent was waiting outside my door to arrest him. He ultimately pled guilty and served a six-month prison term.

What Happened in the Jury Room

To say that I had my hands full as the McDonald trial went on for several weeks outside my office is an understatement.

Occasionally, at night and on weekends, I met with Judge Dupree to talk about some knotty evidentiary issues the trial presented. When the jury returned their verdict of guilty of all three murders, I immediately cleared the jury room and found the ballots.

The jury had voted three times. On the first ballot, they were seven-to-five for conviction; on the second, nine-to-three; and on the third and final vote, they were unanimous.

Unlike current practice in which sentencing usually follows weeks after conviction, at that time, sentencing was instant. Judge Dupree thanked and excused the jury, took a brief recess, and returned to sentence Dr. McDonald to three consecutive life terms. Neither he nor any of my staff in the courtroom had the slightest doubt about guilt.

Judge Dupree explained the sentence of three consecutive life terms privately to me. "This case will never end. It will outlast me," he said. "Another judge can always reduce the sentence, but he cannot increase it."

His prophecy was correct: The case lives on. More than forty years later, I recently testified in Dr. McDonald's third or fourth post-trial motion challenging the verdict.

Chapter 9

—

A Magistrate Judge in the Wild West

"One piece of firewood does not light a fire."
— Zambian proverb

A running theme of my journey is that life unfolds in unexpected ways.

I truly only intended to stay in the Clerk of Court job for two or three years. But things worked out differently. In 1976, Congress passed the Federal Magistrates Act, dramatically expanding the jurisdiction of magistrates (now called magistrate judges) from part-time positions handling small criminal matters into a junior tier of full-fledged federal judges. If the district judges agreed, magistrates could do everything but try felony cases.

Always clever at working systems, Judge Dupree found an obscure provision in the Act that said a clerk of court who otherwise qualified could also be commissioned as a magistrate. Although no legislative history about this provision existed, it was obviously aimed at smaller courts, where some additional help was needed, but not enough to justify a full-time position.

He offered a position of magistrate judge to me, and I jumped at the chance. Although the Administrative Office of the Courts in Washington authorized the appointment and I was approved, there was a problem.

My young age had betrayed me. To be eligible, I had to have been a member of the bar for five years, and I was not quite there.

Both Judge Dupree and I were disappointed. Because of judicial vacancies, the court in those days was slammed with work. "I'll be glad when you grow up and can really help out around here," Judge Dupree frequently muttered. On the fifth anniversary of my bar membership, at age 31, I became eligible.

Joint Appointment in District Court

To make it clear that I had his backing to handle a wide range of matters (and also the backing of Judge Earl Britt, who had joined the court by then), in my first week, Judge Dupree scheduled me to hear a complex summary judgment motion. I looked at the notice and was terrified. The counsel were Howard Manning and McNeil Smith, two of the most respected (and frightening) senior litigators in the state.

I raced down to Judge Dupree's chambers.

"They are going to laugh at this. They won't come to argue to me. I was applying to both of them for jobs not long ago."

He just grinned.

"Get ready and it will work out."

So it did. I held the joint appointment as U.S. Clerk of Court and U.S. Magistrate Judge for 11 years.

It was both exhilarating and exhausting. I carried a full judicial load as a magistrate judge, while also serving as the administrator of the entire court. The magistrate judges handled all of the federal misdemeanors, and a week each month one of us traveled to Fayetteville to handle the huge criminal docket off of Fort Bragg.

WELCOME TO THE WILD WEST

The federal courtroom in Fayetteville was the Wild West. It is the biggest in the country, and it was packed the entire week. I calculated that to get through a day, I had to handle a case every 90 seconds.

My different roles were often overlapping and sometimes confusing – to me and others. For instance, I was bothered by the starkness of the lobby outside our Raleigh courtrooms. I ordered planters to soften the space. Then I discovered that according to the byzantine rules of my budget, I could pay for planters and plants, but not for a service contract to maintain them. No problem. My primary hobby is gardening, so I just took care of the plants myself.

One Friday afternoon I was working in the lobby with my clippers and watering can. A guard from the state prison was sitting there waiting on a prisoner who was inside the courtroom testifying. Inside the courtroom, the marshals took custody. When the guard was sure it was only the two of us in earshot, he walked over to me and said in a low voice, "What happened to you, boy?"

I said I wasn't sure what he meant.

"Last time I brought someone over here to testify, you were the judge."

THE FATALISM OF A JUDGE

Judges in every democracy share a fatalism about the risks to their personal safety. But it's more pronounced in our country than throughout Africa. There, a disgruntled litigant probably doesn't have access to a firearm. Still, courthouses are where dreams die, often leaving litigants embittered. During my career I've watched the federal courts in this nation transition from buildings with open and unrestricted access to controlled fortresses.

In recent years, judges and families have been horrifically murdered, virtually every time away from the courthouse.

Therein comes the fatalism. As secure as we are in our buildings, we walk out the door completely unprotected. In trying to keep renovation costs down, I questioned whether the huge cost of bulletproof glass in my courtroom was necessary. I was assured it was, as snipers on an adjacent roof could pick me off on the bench.

I suggested they look at the unprotected parking lot below.

"Why wouldn't they just wait until I am walking to my car?"

This was brought home to me late in my judicial career. I was in the midst of a huge case. A technology company had declared bankruptcy, just as some valuable intellectual property it spent years developing was ready to hit the market. The investors were livid, expecting they were victims of a "patent bustout," in which the insiders cleverly bought the intellectual property from the bankruptcy trustee and squeezed out all of their investors.

One of my law clerks, Blake Boyette, came into my chambers. He was as pale as a sheet.

"I think you just got a death threat," he said. "Some guy who sounded like (Arnold) Schwarzenegger said to give you a message. He said if you do not rule correctly today, it has been arranged for you to be shot dead through the head."

Since many of the investors were European, this rung authentic.

"Where's the ambiguity?" I said to Blake, picking up the phone to call the U.S. Marshal. Threats against judges are common-place, and I got my fair share. Most, thankfully, were idle.

The U.S. Marshal's Service has a sophisticated assessment protocol, during which they determine the severity of a threat and organize a response. Late that afternoon, word came back from D.C. to lock down my family and me at the highest level of security.

By then, my oldest daughter and I were on a plane to Chicago to spend the weekend with one of my older sons and his family. My wife and two younger children were stunned when the marshals moved in, using our dining room as a command post and ac-companying them everywhere they went. One of our watchful neighbors, Elizabeth Manning, called to ask, "Whitney, why are big burly men walking around your yard?"

Saturday afternoon, my wife, who has a unique sense of humor, called.

"Target, we're at the pool with our marshal, Raymond. He's in a suit and clearly packing. Cain (who was three at the time) is introducing him to everyone as his new friend who lives with us. Any special way you want me to play this?"

Mine it for all it was worth, I told her.

A marshal's convoy met my older daughter and me at the airport, and they stayed with us for another week. At that point, they determined by whom and from where the call originated, and again thankfully, it came from Europe. The caller was placed on the "no fly" list until he could be more formally charged. I worried needlessly about the effects of the experience on my children. The morning after protection ended, Cain raced downstairs and returned again dejected.

"Where is my police?" he said.

"It Will Get Me, Too"

We were safe — physically, anyway — and we continued with our lives, including hosting African guests as we had for years. Some of our visits, though, had unexpected consequences.

A delegation of court administrators from Tanzania spent a week with me in Raleigh, making several visits to our home. One of the young registrars, Joyce, got on extremely well with my wife. Some weeks later, we received what we thought would be a thank you note.

Instead, it was a serious request to return to the United States as my second wife, a position tolerated by the customary law in many African countries. She outlined all of the services she would provide and gave us her understanding that she would be completely under the direction of and subservient to my spouse.

We demurred. Soon to have three babies in less than four years, Whitney would later wonder if we had made a mistake in declining her offer.

Other visits had sad endings.

One of the strategies to improve case management was identifying bright, talented young administrators and bringing them to the United States for intense tutorials. After several trips to Zambia, I identified a young assistant registrar, John, as a man of great promise who could possibly, someday, move up to a top position in the national court.

Similarly, a young woman named Maggie was a natural with computers and could be elevated to be an IT director. Both served stints in various U.S. courts, including mine.

Within a year, I got a cryptic message.

"I am sad to tell you that John died of a brief illness."

It was shorthand for succumbing to AIDS. Within six months, the same message came about Maggie. I saw the devastation caused by AIDS on the continent. My embassy driver was a lovely young guy, the youngest of six siblings. He was the only one still surviving and was struggling to support twenty-one nieces and nephews on his driver's salary.

He was also fatalistic.

"It will get me, too. And then they will have no one."

Chapter 10

—

A Courthouse with Great Bones

"When you run alone, you run fast.
When you run together, you run far."
— African proverb

I'm a history buff, and I was eager to see the courthouses in Africa. They ran the gamut. The Supreme Court of Zambia was a majestic building with great bones that had fallen on hard times. Originally built as a symbol of colonial power, it had spacious courtrooms and gracious chambers.

Zambia, too, had fallen on hard times, and maintenance money was sparse. The old, stately courthouse was now rundown and shabby. In fact, I never did find a working men's toilet there, necessitating frequent trips back to my hotel.

In contrast, the new Supreme Court building in Namibia is one of the most striking architectural structures I've ever seen.

Architectural Jewel in Raleigh

One of my responsibilities as Clerk I most enjoyed was the maintenance and care of the federal courthouses across eastern

North Carolina. The majestic building on the Cape Fear River in Wilmington is now more than a hundred years old. During criminal trials for the importation of marijuana, the drug boats were tied at the dock in front, on display for juries to see. The courthouse had double banks of windows rising to a forty-foot ceiling, covered with an intricate plaster design.

Sadly, in the 1950s, the government landlord, GSA, in an ill-designed energy project, dropped in a fake acoustical tile ceiling above the first tier of windows, giving the room the squashed appearance of a Walmart. When the roof started to leak, I conspired with a young GSA architect to rip out the fake ceiling and uncover the cause. I made the case that it was cheaper to restore it to its original grandeur than to replace the cheap ceiling.

The courthouses in Elizabeth City and New Bern are equally magnificent.

In Fayetteville, the federal courthouse is cavernous rather than elegant, designed to accommodate the huge volume of criminal traffic from Fort Bragg (the Wild West, remember).

Sadly, in Raleigh, the main federal courthouse in the district is a nondescript, eight story white box, built in the utilitarian style of the 1960s.

The courthouse I know most intimately is the jewel of the lot, the Century Station Federal Building in downtown Raleigh. The first federal courthouse built in North Carolina after the Civil War, it was the headquarters for the federal courts until they outgrew it and moved to the aforementioned white box. Part of the national building boom after the Civil War, it is simply stunning.

But after the federal courts left, the building fell into complete disrepair. In 2005, our bankruptcy court grew from two to three judges, and I was able to surrender my small courthouse in Wilson to the new judge from Greenville. Although a colleague occupied the second-floor courtroom and chambers, the top two floors were vacant and in disrepair. Some of the rooms hadn't been occupied since the 1960s. Ceilings had fallen in. The original wooden floors were infested with termites, and the once-elegant spaces were haphazardly divided into cubicles. During one of our regular North Carolina hurricanes, I spent the weekend in the building emptying trash cans of water that poured through the ceiling.

I set about bringing this grand old building back.

Turns out there were 76 boxes of construction documents in the National Archives in Washington, chronicling daily activity on the structure from 1872 to 1876. These documents told the story of a stately building with sixteen marble fireplaces, mahogany and walnut-trimmed paneling, and gorgeous gas chandeliers. Back then, the citizenry was intrigued by the novelty of locking postal boxes, as well as the first indoor toilets in Raleigh for the judge and marshal. Eventually, I connected the dots.

This was a Mullett building!

Alfred Mullett was the supervising architect of the treasury after the Civil War, and he was responsible for all federal construction. Mullett personally designed more than 50 buildings, and Century Station is one of only fourteen remaining. When the history office of GSA in Atlanta finally figured this out, money flowed liberally. I spent three years camped in a first-floor office using borrowed courtrooms as we painstakingly brought the building back to its former greatness.

The fireplaces were a problem. Federal building rules permit a fireplace to be restored, but not built anew. I recall the day jubilant workers charged into my courtroom to tell me they had finally broken through a plaster wall into a 140-year-old firebox. Now we could rebuild a fireplace according to the original design.

THE GHOST OF ALFRED MULLETT

I grew close to the workmen, who told me about the strange things that happened at the site. As they sat on the floor eating lunch, a broom would suddenly hurl across the room. Closed doors and windows would come open when no one was present. Most striking of all, one day at dusk, as they were headed to the elevator lobby, the workers looked back and saw a tall, bearded man in a long coat at the end of the hall. We had had trouble with vagrants, and as they started down the hall to ask him to leave, he disappeared into thin air. When I showed them a picture of Alfred Mullett, they blanched.

"That was him."

Although not my office any longer, the building remains a showpiece of the federal judiciary. I am pleased to have helped restore its original luster.

WRITING THE RULES IN ZAMBIA

After about a dozen trips to Zambia, my work there was coming to a natural close. We had improved case management systems and implemented some basic automation.

And we had taken on one other project.

Although the British had modernized their incredibly complex

High Court rules dating back to the nineteenth century, the Zambians had not. The simplest of cases became enmeshed in the complexities of British pleading rules.

With some encouragement, the Chief Justice had appointed a High Court Rules Committee, and I was named its Reporter. Over a couple of years, we completely revised and simplified the High Court Rules of Zambia, and the Parliament approved them.

It was a satisfying end to that phase of my African journey.

Part 2
Tanzania

—

*"Every traveler has a home of his own,
and he learns to appreciate it the
more from his wandering."*

Charles Dickens

Chapter 11

—

The Unique Pleasure of
Bankruptcy Court

*The U.S. Bankruptcy Act of 1898 (the Nelson Act) established a
uniform system of bankruptcy throughout the United States.*

But it was not to be the end of my time in Africa.

This was so because the Chief Justice of Zambia proudly
boasted to the Chief Justice of Tanzania about the fine work he
and I had been doing.

And just like that, I found myself pivoting countries and
entering the orbit of one of the finest and smartest people
with whom I have ever worked, the venerable Chief Justice of
Tanzania, Francis Nyalali. He served as Chief Justice through
threats of military coups, socialist regimes, dictatorships, and
democratically elected governments. In fact, the only constant
in Tanzania for decades was his comforting presence in power.
At 23 years, his term remains the longest of any chief justice in
the British Commonwealth.

To understand court administration in Africa, you have to know
a bit of history.

Today, Tanzania is a bustling tropical nation of 44 million people. Before World War I, it was called German East Africa, brutally administered by its German overseers. At the end of the war, Germany relinquished all its overseas colonies. The name became Tanganyika, and the League of Nations assigned it to Great Britain as a protectorate. The United Nations continued this arrangement after World War II.

Increasing pressure for independence during the 1950s was finally successful in 1961. Zanzibar was a separate protectorate under Great Britain and was given its independence in 1963 as a constitutional monarchy under its Sultan.

But the African majority revolted against its new ruler, and in 1964, Tanganyika and Zanzibar united to form Tanzania.

The father of Tanzania was Julius Nyere, who held power from independence until 1985. Since then, the country has changed presidents peacefully with democratic elections, but with very different political philosophies.

All of that tumult occurred within a relatively short span of years, so it is little wonder their judicial systems lag behind ours in many respects.

No Way to Choose Judges

But one way in which Africa is miles ahead of us is how it selects its judges.

Particularly in our federal courts, the path to a judgeship has become a gruesome gauntlet. At times, a political litmus test has become more important than integrity and competence. In many of our state courts, judges barely have time to take their seats before they must run again in lengthy, expensive, and increasingly partisan campaigns.

It was refreshing to see how differently, and cleanly, it's done in Africa.

Judicial selection in each country falls under a constitutionally required Judicial Service Commission. Zambia is a good example. There, the Commission is chaired by the chief justice and includes a supreme court justice, the attorney general, the solicitor general, a member of parliament, the dean of the law school, the president of the Law Association, the secretary to the cabinet, the chair of the Public Service Commission, and a legal practitioner. When a vacancy occurs in the Supreme or the High Court, this Commission sends a name to the president for his nomination, who must then be confirmed by Parliament. With regard to the Subordinate Court, the Commission itself selects the magistrates.

This seems to work smoothly across Africa and ensures the most competent judges are both recruited from the bar and promoted from within. The members of the Commission are of such stature that their opinions are respected and, more importantly, because the membership is by position rather than individual, it can't be rigged by an appointing authority to its own advantage.

It's a sane, civilized process. We could learn a lot from it.

ON THE BANKRUPTCY BENCH

In 1991, a sudden vacancy occurred on the U.S. Bankruptcy Court in our district when Judge Thomas Moore died unexpectedly. Judge Moore was almost larger than life. He was the first bankruptcy judge in our district after the 1979 Act created the position. He was also a general in the Air Force Reserve and a forceful presence fiercely devoted to his staff and bar. In exchange, he had his people's complete affection and loyalty.

As a striking example of how that Wilson, N.C., native could get things done, he singlehandedly persuaded Congress to build a single-judge courthouse as headquarters of the court in our district.

In 1991, Judge Moore became ill with a resistant case of pneumonia. Just before he died, doctors, to their horror, discovered the pneumonia was masking an undiagnosed case of tuberculosis.

That is why when I'm asked how, considering my background, I became a bankruptcy judge, I perhaps too flippantly answer: "Bad health care in Wilson County."

Bankruptcy judges are picked through the cleanest merit process we have in this country. A statutory merit selection panel takes applications and sends the top candidates to the regional court of appeals. That court is required to pick from the list. The process is quick, fair, and confidential.

I decided to go for it. I tossed my hat into the ring for U.S. Bankruptcy Court Judge.

I was ready for a change. Preferring civil litigation, I was weary of the countless hours in the courtroom the criminal docket of a magistrate judge required. Another factor: In 1991, President George H.W. Bush held an 80 percent approval rating. I didn't think another Democratic president would ever come along who might consider me for a lifetime judicial appointment.

So I became a U.S. Bankruptcy Court Judge in the summer of 1992. It was rough going at first. I didn't know much about bankruptcy law. Every day was an intense seminar. I was a stranger to the bankruptcy bar and staff and seen as a bit of an imposter. My casual informality could not have been more different from the military bearing of my predecessor, and it rattled folks.

PLEASE RESIGN

The bankruptcy courts have huge dockets and process thousands of orders daily. Many of these are routine, but I asked to see everything issued in my name until I fully understood what was going on. I was often at the courthouse until midnight, going through stacks of motions and proposed orders.

One night, as I was nearing the end of a stack, I found someone had slipped a sheet of legal paper into the pile and anonymously written, "You should resign."

My first impulse was to ignore it. But after a worried and sleepless night, I showed it to my able clerk of court, Peggy Deans. She was horrified and promised to get to the bottom of it. She returned a few minutes later, laughing so hard she could not catch her breath.

"It says re-sign," she explained. "The copier ate the orders below this yesterday, and you need to sign these again."

I came to adore every part of being a bankruptcy judge. In contrast to the myth that it's a narrow and specialized area, a claim in bankruptcy can arise in any area of law. I was constantly dipping into substantive areas I knew nothing about. The docket was incredibly varied, from a single mother with a mobile home full of children trying to hang on, to an airline that had run into financial difficulty.

In addition, the Eastern District is a big place, with lots of different locations where the statute commands us to hold court. My colleague, the legendary Tom Small, was our Chief Judge, and he handled Raleigh and Fayetteville. I took the rest of the district and rode circuit from the small Wilson courthouse I inherited to New Bern, Wilmington, Greenville, and Elizabeth City.

One of my first law clerks, Bob Gourley, was once asked why he loved his job so much. He replied, "Because it has so many weekends." It seemed that every Monday, we were loading up to travel to a different city to start a session Tuesday morning.

ARGUE WITH ME, PLEASE

Every day I realized how lucky I was to have such a remarkable staff. Over more than two decades I had more than fifty law clerks, often choosing from several hundred applications.

One of my first instructions to all law clerks was this: Argue with me.

"You are the only thing between me and a bad mistake."

One clerk, Dave Lambert, took this instruction to a whole new level.

Dave spent his first day trying to understand the consequences of a complex business transaction that had completely unraveled. Late in the afternoon, I announced my ruling from the bench. Turning to Dave as we left the courtroom, I asked him what he thought. Without hesitation, he said, "You completely fucked that up." After substantial conversation, he began to see the legal issues my way. When Dave tells that story, he says the typical response is that he was lucky to clerk for the only federal judge in the country who would not have shown him the door for saying such a thing. But our relationship deepened into more than just a professional one. A few years later, I flew to Ireland to officiate at his wedding, courtesy of a one-day commission from the Irish High Court to sit as a judge there.

Many of the cases I heard in bankruptcy court involved farmers, whose financial fortunes rose and fell with hurricanes, droughts, and price fluctuations. Lawyers who appeared in my court were surprised to find I was not the city slicker they expected, but had actually primed tobacco, cut silage, and baled hay. I stopped one proceeding to ask the assembled courtroom, "Would everyone here who has ever ridden a combine raise your hand?" Two did: the farmer on the witness stand and me.

Central to my years as a bankruptcy judge was my courtroom deputy, Felecia Lucas. A regal woman of color, she could command a courtroom with a single, stern look. Though I am accurately seen as being informal personally, as a judge I ran a completely formal courtroom. No one spoke but the lawyers in the case, the witness on the stand, and me.

Felecia was there to enforce that rule.

Whispering lawyers would say they suddenly perceived the eye of God upon them and would look up to see Felecia glaring. In my early days, it took us a while to get our bearing. After I finished a classic "he-said-she-said" trial, during which one of the witnesses was totally lying, I asked her opinion. She demurred.

"You're the judge. It's not proper for me to say." When I suggested otherwise, she replied, "Well, OK then. That hussy is lying through her teeth." I thought so also. From then on, Felecia and I were an inseparable team.

Chapter 12

—

A Brutal Dive into Federal Judicial Politics

"Procuring an Article III federal judicial nomination is a massive political campaign without rules."

In 1992, the political landscape shifted when 12 years of Republican presidents ended with the election of Bill Clinton. My professional prospects changed too. Although my time at Yale Law briefly overlapped with President Clinton's, I did not know him. But I had many friends who did.

Simultaneously, two North Carolina seats had become open on the U.S. Court of Appeals for the Fourth Circuit – one from the retirement of the venerated Judge Dickson Phillips, and a new seat from expansion of the size of the Court from 12 to 15. The Fourth Circuit had no diversity at that time, so it was a given that Clinton would use one seat to cure that problem. The other was up for grabs, and I was interested.

There were any number of more prominent Democratic lawyers in the state, but most had baggage. They had either been involved in controversial cases or supported and funded Democratic candidates.

And the political situation was complex. North Carolina had two conservative Republican senators: Jesse Helms and Lauch Faircloth. To further complicate matters, in 1994, the Republicans reclaimed the Senate and restored the primacy of the blue slip, meaning a home state senator had an absolute veto over any nomination.

Still, I thought I might be the dark horse who could slip through.

Unlike putting your name in the hat for a bankruptcy judgeship, procuring an Article III federal judicial nomination is a massive political campaign without rules. With a briefing book of several hundred pages, I began soliciting support. It was two-pronged. First, I had to be the choice of the North Carolina Democratic political establishment. Second, I had to clear the White House selection criteria, which, for appellate judges, is incredibly high.

Normally, the senator of the president's party would be the clearinghouse, but we had none. So, the White House turned to Governor Jim Hunt for a recommendation. Hunt, in turn, put his chief of staff, Brad Wilson, in charge. I procured hundreds of letters of support from both sides of the aisle. I had spent a career trying to be a fair and transparent court administrator and judge, and it paid off.

When I was surprised at the enthusiastic support a conservative lawyer gave me, he reminded me of an incident years earlier.

"I called you in desperation when you were the Clerk of Court because I was not going to get a brief in a major case filed by the court's closing time. You calmed me down by saying if I could get it to your house by midnight, you would file it at your dining room table and it would be timely. I was there at 11:30. I never forgot."

CLINTON WHITE HOUSE TROIKA

The Clinton White House used a troika to pick appellate judges, a group led by Judge Abner Mikva, the White House Counsel.

I knew Judge Mikva, as we had worked extensively together on a commission dealing with the dry (but actually fascinating) topic of the rules for retention of federal court records.

The other two on the selection team were Associate White House Counsel Vickie Radd and Associate Attorney General Eleanor Acheson. I knew neither. Worse yet, both had gone to Harvard.

But I was cheered when I looked into their backgrounds. Vickie Radd had practiced law with one of my good law school buddies, Judy Miller. Judy had actually been her supervising partner. A quick call to Judy put me in play. Similarly, Eleanor Acheson had taught at Georgetown Law in the office adjacent to another close buddy, Vicki Jackson. Another phone call was made.

Later, when folks asked in amazement how I managed to secure this nomination, I would reply, "In school I always liked the really smart girls. They turned out to be running the country."

Although I thought things were proceeding nicely, I was taken aback by a call from the White House. With no Republican senators, the caller said, they would like to see more support from the Democratic congressional delegation. I thought for a moment, then smiled and made another call. During my break from law school to finish a master's degree in education, my clinical placement had been as a guidance counselor in a rural Cabarrus County elementary school. A bright young seventh-grader named Stacy Heffner was a frequent visitor to my office.

I called Stacy.

A couple of days later, one of my puzzled law clerks came into my office. "I just got a call. This woman said to tell Mr. Leonard it's OK with daddy and OK with Charlie. What does that mean?"

I said, "It means that North Carolina's two senior Democratic congressmen just called the White House and endorsed me."

Stacy Heffner Rose was the daughter of Congressman Bill Heffner and married to Congressman Charlie Rose. A double dose of good fortune.

So that part worked out well.

Then in December of 1995, President Clinton sent my nomination, together with that of Judge Jim Beatty, a federal district judge in Winston-Salem, to the Senate. Jim would be the first African-American judge on the court, and his nomination drew more press attention. Interestingly, Jim and I are the same age. We both grew up in Davidson County and graduated from high schools at opposite ends of the county in the same year.

Even so, my nomination was noticed, especially among the bankruptcy community. It was the first time a president had ever nominated a bankruptcy judge straight to a court of appeals without a stop at a district court.

PLAYING THE CONFIRMATION GAME

The confirmation process is chaotic. You receive exhaustive and inconsistent questionnaires to complete from the FBI, the Justice Department, the Senate Judiciary Committee, and the American Bar Association. FBI agents fan out to interview a bewildering array of acquaintances. My doctor, an Indian national, was terrified when FBI agents showed up at his office to demand a copy of my medical records. The marriage counselor with whom my first wife and I had met couldn't believe she had to submit to an interview.

One question in particular required enormous work. I had to disclose and provide a copy of any opinion I ever wrote involving a constitutional issue. Prisoners assert constitutional claims in the federal courts by the hundreds of thousands. As a magistrate judge I had dealt with hundreds. A squadron of former law clerks and I spent night after night going through the district court order books to find and copy any opinion meeting that description.

As intrusive as it is, I don't object to this level of scrutiny. Federal judges are critically important to our constitutional democracy. I've watched dozens of men and women ascend to these positions, and in virtually every instance they become nobler and better people. But in that rare instance when we get it wrong, it is a disaster.

The selection is rightly arduous, in my view.

Luckily for me, this was in 1995, before federal judicial confirmations became guerilla warfare. It was the rule back then that if you were a qualified candidate and the president's choice, it worked out.

Again, I was hopeful as I met with my two senators.

Senator Faircloth could not have been more hospitable. At the end of the conversation, though, he said he would follow "Jesse's lead on this."

Senator Helms was a different story. Courteous in his courtly Southern way, he nonetheless told me he just couldn't see ever supporting a nomination of this President. The situation was not helped by the fact he thought he had been double-crossed by Senators Joe Biden and Terry Sanford in the last days of the Bush

Administration on one of his nominations. He was still chapped.

But I refused to give up easily, and I pulled out all the stops.

Judge Frank Dupree, a fellow Republican and close friend of Helms, wrote him at least a dozen times asking him to relent. If anyone could get Jesse to change his mind on me, it was my mentor and the judge I clerked for.

Another heavyweight, University of North Carolina system President Bill Friday, who grew up with Helms in the same small town, flew to Washington to advocate on my behalf.

Editorials and cartoons denounced Helm's stonewalling.

For all that, it was not meant to be.

Nominations die when a Senate session adjourns *sine die*. When the Republicans kept Senate control in the 1996 elections, I declined to be renominated. Twisting in the wind was too much of a diversion from my otherwise rich life, and I wanted no more of it. Senator Helms was true to his word, and he also blocked Judge Jim Beatty, then Judge Jim Wynn, and also Professor Elizabeth Gibson.

When Judge Sam Ervin died in 1999, all three of the North Carolina seats on the Court of Appeals became vacant for years. As the biggest state in the circuit, this was a travesty. But Helms could have cared less.

Once Again, into the Breach

As much as I would have enjoyed a seat on the Court of Appeals, the position I wanted more than any other was as a federal district judge in Raleigh.

A path opened in 1999. My close friend John Edwards unexpectedly upset Senator Faircloth and was now the junior senator from North Carolina. Usually, a candidate who is the choice of the president and the senator of the president's party is a slam dunk. Senator Sanford once told me he had deferred to six of Senator Helms' picks under this rule, although he was not happy about some of them. Judge Earl Britt had taken senior status at the very young age of 65 and created a vacancy.

The White House told me I was the presumptive choice, and again began my background check.

It almost derailed over a transaction between John and me years earlier. I had sunk into a deep depression when my first marriage unraveled in the summer of 1994. John decided I could run myself out of it, so he forced me to train with him for a marathon. Running myself into exhaustion every day did not cure hopeless insomnia. One afternoon in the middle of a trial, I crashed. I told my law clerk, "I just can't go back in there. Tell the counsel I have suddenly become ill and am taking a recess." I called my wonderful internist in Raleigh, Dr. Anant Soni, and said, "I am headed to your office and will wait until you can see me."

Pharmaceuticals helped, and I began to get back on my feet, but that did not cure my major problem. My brilliant oldest son, Matt, wanted to go to Yale and had gained early admission. It made sense, as he had been born in New Haven and both of his parents graduated from law school there. His tuition was due, and I simply did not have my half to pay. There was significant equity tied up in various real estate we had always intended to use to educate our sons, but it was jointly titled, and I could not reach it. I was at my wit's end.

John left me a message that said, "Go by my house and get an envelope out of the mailbox. I can't stand to see you like this."

I did, and in it was a check for $25,000, with a note to "pay me back when you can." It was a supreme gesture of friendship that put me back on course. In 1998, when my second son was finishing college, I refinanced my home and repaid the money.

The White House was completely baffled by this transaction. How a loan to me years earlier from my then unknown but millionaire friend could have influenced a nomination five years later was not clear to me. But still, they thought it odd. They made me retain a private tax attorney to give them an opinion letter saying it was an arm's-length loan paid back appropriately. They were surprised to find I accurately disclosed the loan on every one of my judicial financial disclosure statements required to be filed annually. At one point, I said in exasperation, "Don't any of you people have friends?"

I got nominated.

It should have been easier. I had total support of the North Carolina Bar from all quarters, and again, the highly sought-after unanimous "well qualified" rating from the American Bar Association. The idea I could follow in Judge Dupree's legacy and join men I loved and respected – Earl Britt, Jim Fox, and Mac Howard – on their court was a life's dream.

Yet I underestimated how brutal North Carolina judicial politics had become and remains today. Immediately, the conservative staff around Senator Helms agreed on a strategy to block my nomination without challenging me personally. In fact, they could not say enough nice things about my qualifications. It was just that according to the Chief Judge, the workload of the court did not justify another judge, and it was a waste of taxpayer money to confirm me. Senator Helms turned me into the "million-dollar judge" who was not necessary, and again held my blue slip on this pretense. He actually introduced legislation to strip the Eastern District of the judgeship and transfer it to the Western District, where he said it was more needed. Of course, this nonsense disappeared a year later when the second President Bush won, and they immediately began to campaign for one of their own to get the vacant seat.

There's a surprising postscript to this saga. A couple of weeks after President George W. Bush took office, I got a call from the White House asking if I could be in Washington the next day to meet with Justice Alberto Gonzalez, the new White House counsel. When they asked if I knew where to go, I assured them I had been there ... often. My courtesy interview with Justice Gonzalez stretched to two hours, and we hit it off. Ironically, we are both now law school deans.

Gonzalez told me the President was irritated at this North Carolina nonsense and was going to end it. He had told Senators Helms and Edwards to each put up candidates he could review. Gonzalez was having the same conversation with my buddy, Judge Jim Wynn. We were both told this was a done deal and one of us would get the nod shortly. The call never came. To this day, Jim and I greet each other with, "Did they call you?"

It turned out that now with a Republican president, Senator Helms insisted he should get both picks.

Thankfully, Judge Wynn finally made it to the federal bench with an Obama appointment. By that point I had turned 60 and was no longer under consideration.

My disappointment over these experiences was largely assuaged because throughout this period I continued to use all my discretionary time to return to Africa two or three times a year.

Chapter 13

—

Dar Es Salaam

"A roaring lion catches no game."
— Tanzanian proverb

My first day in Dar es Salaam, I met a remarkable woman who was to become a great friend. My State Department liaison there, Kiki Munshi, was one of our senior diplomats, a tall, statuesque woman with a strong voice and infectious laugh. She commanded any room she entered. This put her in good stead when, years later, she was pulled out of retirement to be the Head of a Provincial Reconstruction Team in Iraq during our military occupation.

Never has a name so mismatched a person; she should have been an Eleanor or Josephine. She lived in a spacious mansion that was part of the American diplomatic compound on the Indian Ocean, and her seven guest rooms housed a bizarre and ever-changing assortment of visitors, artists, diplomats, expatriates, and friends. Official guests like me often stayed there to minimize lodging expenses. It was the most fascinating place I ever stayed.

Kiki threw you right in. After my first exhausting Monday visiting the court where I would be working, I returned to her office for a ride home. She left a note: "Detained at a meeting. Take the car and go home." I had only the vaguest idea where home was, but a cleaner gave me some basic directions.

Driving in a congested African capital at rush hour is not easy for anyone. I soon found myself in the inner lane of a four-lane roundabout, going the wrong way for me (Tanzanians drive on the left side.) I was stuck there for about 45 minutes, until I finally just laid on the horn and made a dash for it. Amid much squealing of brakes, I made it out and found her house by using the seagulls as my beacon.

No More "Death by Hanging"

Chief Justice Nyalali – who had served for years under the most trying of circumstances – was a true citizen of the world and fascinated by computers. He was convinced that automation was the answer to his backlog. At his request, the World Bank bought the Court a roomful of computers. A team of German programmers who weren't lawyers and knew nothing about common law courts had come before me to work on a case management system with the Tanzanians, who in turn had never seen a computer and had no idea why they were being asked these questions. The programmers were trained to keep asking questions, and the Tanzanians, by nature, continued to answer them politely.

The result was garbage.

As an example, they had identified forty different ways a civil case could terminate in Tanzania, most of them just synonyms without any legal meaning. The last was "death by hanging," just to be sure all bases were covered. We immediately cut the number of case conclusions to nine, each represented by a numerical code from one to nine.

One of the programs we developed in Tanzania was a simple piece of scheduling software showing the trial calendars for all of the High Court judges. The Chief Justice was so proud of this new system he assembled his entire bench in his chambers for a demonstration. I first pulled up the calendar of the only woman judge on the high court. Her calendar was jammed. Morning and afternoon sessions, five days a week, an impossible caseload.

Next, I pulled up the calendar for the senior male judge on the Court. When his schedule appeared, I thought the software had malfunctioned. A straight line appeared down the middle of the screen. We all had the same stunned reaction as we realized he only held court on Wednesdays.

It was the most vivid display of the power of automation I've ever seen. The Chief Justice looked at the judge with the light schedule sternly and said: "I now see why My Lady is so fatigued. She will not be fatigued any longer."

HAUNCH OF IMPALA

That Saturday night, Kiki invited a number of the Tanzanian judges and court administrators with whom I was working to dinner. I assumed her cook would take care of the meal. When I came downstairs on Saturday morning, there was another note: "Out at all-day meeting. You say you're a cook, do something with this for dinner."

Next to the note was a frozen haunch of impala.

Being from North Carolina, I had at least a vague notion of how to prepare the impala. I spent the morning defrosting it in hot water, then cut it into cubes, marinated it in a tangy, homemade barbecue sauce, and made kabobs to grill. Served over herbed rice, it was delicious. Our guests agreed it was better than the goat they had brought, which was a bit dry. With the sides that Kiki and her cook prepared, it was a delightful meal under the moonlight beside the Indian Ocean.

THE PARADISE OF STONE TOWN IN ZANZIBAR

Through Kiki, I met her friend Emerson, an expatriate Virginian who with his partner ran a hotel in Zanzibar. A big-hearted guy who enjoyed having another Southerner around, Emerson and I got on famously. I eagerly accepted his invitation to visit for the weekend.

That first trip to Zanzibar was a nightmare.

To encourage tourism, the Tanzanian government had invested heavily in a couple of high-speed hydrofoils designed to whisk you across the strait separating Dar es Salaam from Zanzibar in less than an hour. Unfortunately, on my trip, only one of the four engines were working, and we chugged along in a turbulent sea more like a tugboat. Huge waves crashed into the big windows designed for pleasant sightseeing. At times we came close to capsizing. It was like spending three hours in a washing machine. Everyone on the boat upchucked and I spent the next day flat on my back trying to recover from a near fatal case of seasickness.

When I recovered, I strolled out into a paradise.

Stone Town in Zanzibar may be the most fascinating place on earth, built over centuries aside the Indian Ocean. Its winding streets, with no perceptible layout, are so narrow in places you can stretch your arms and touch the buildings on both sides.

The first floor of each building is invariably a shop supporting the family that lives above. The island has a rich history as a commercial center, still today producing much of the spice used throughout the world. In a darker time, it was the center of the Arab slave trade. More slaves transited through Zanzibar headed into the Arab world than left through the Gold Coast headed to the western world.

EMERSON THE EXPATRIATE HOTELIER

Emerson's hotel in Zanzibar was stunning. Each room was uniquely restored with indigenous furniture, linens, and art. The rooftop restaurant, where you sat on Persian rugs and looked out over the moonlit Indian Ocean, regularly appeared in travel magazines as one of the most romantic spots in the world.

Emerson made me a proposition. South of Zanzibar is Chole, an island inhabited for centuries by its own Swahili tribe. There is no development whatsoever, but Emerson had negotiated a deal with the tribe to build them a small infirmary in exchange for being allowed to establish a small, tented tourist camp. The camp was finished but had not opened. He invited me to come back the next weekend for a dry run. Victor, a student intern from North Texas University, was working in Tanzania at the time, and I invited him to come along.

Emerson arranged everything. The next Friday afternoon we flew to Zanzibar and met a jeep. A driver took us to the very south end of Zanzibar. Right on schedule appeared our dhow, a wooden sailing vessel and the staple of Indian Ocean commerce for centuries. The sailors aboard spoke no English, and my Swahili consisted of a few directional phrases.

Without hesitating, we jumped in.

It was Peter Pan and the lost boys. We sailed into our own small harbor with the tent camp on a rise above us. Through hand gestures we understood that we were to disembark, but that the boat would return the next day. After we picked our tents and settled in, we realized that a Swahili lady had quietly appeared and was cooking a fabulous dinner of fresh fish. After she cleaned up and departed, we saw she had left a bottle of Konyagi, the fabulous local gin, and two glasses on the table. We managed to kill it.

The next morning, our dhow reappeared in the harbor, and we climbed aboard. We sailed about a mile out to the world-famous barrier reef and snorkeled all day. In the water, close to us at all times, was a native swimmer with a long spear. We realized later it was our shark protection. We returned at dusk to repeat the elegant dinner and to down another bottle of gin.

For the return trip, Emerson told us, our friends with the dhow would take us back to Zanzibar. A four-seater plane would land there to fly us back to Dar. The plan sounded dubious, and the plane was late. Finally, it broke through the clouds and came down on the dirt runway. Two young boys jumped out, followed by their dad, the pilot. We hopped in the back two seats, the boys strapped into the co-pilot seat, and we made the quick return trip to the mainland.

SUB-SAHARAN COURT AUTOMATION PROJECT

Chief Justice Nyalali was so thrilled with the results of our court automation project that he eagerly sought opportunities to show it off. He asked the American ambassador to underwrite a conference he would host on case management for all of the sub-Saharan chief justices. Each chief justice would be invited to present a paper about initiatives in his own country, but the showpiece was to be my live demonstration of the results of the Tanzanian project.

To our amazement and delight, fifteen chief justices accepted the invitation and came.

Now we had to put on a show. This took meticulous planning. Hierarchy and rank are important on that continent, so careful thought went into such things as assignment of hotel rooms and cars, and the order in which the cars would depart and return. I distinctly recall the condescension the white chief justice of Zimbabwe showed to his black African colleagues. No matter what was said, he would claim it was done better in Zimbabwe.

That was true at the time. Zimbabwe was the breadbasket of Africa, and Harare rivaled Capetown in sophistication. In a chilling example of how quickly an autocrat can destroy a nation, within a few years the Chief Justice and his entire court were deposed. With his seizure and redistribution of land, President Robert Mugabe in a few short years reduced the entire nation to penury and made it a pariah in the world community.

Needless to say, I was nervous as our big automation conference approached. The event was held in a large convention center, and we jerry-rigged all the electronics and screens for the demonstration. The power supply in Dar was never stable, and I knew a sudden surge could undo the entire presentation. Sure enough, I was halfway through my remarks when the screen went dark. Chief Justice Nyalali was rattled. He was soon to step down as Chief Justice and this conference was his crowning achievement. Although I have never actually wet my pants from stress, that was the closest I ever came. It turned out that a late arrival had tripped over a cord and unplugged it. This was easily remedied, and we continued without incident.

The response to the conference was enthusiastic. I received multiple requests from the chief justices assembled there to work in their countries.

I picked what was to become my absolute favorite African country: Namibia.

Chapter 14

—

I Killed Jubilee

"If tall blond boys with thick drawls from Little Rock and Welcome are leading the protests, this war is almost over."

In every country I visited, I made a point of visiting the universities where their lawyers were trained. The sprawling and attractive campus of the University of Zambia was always largely empty, wracked with dissension, with some group or another always boycotting or on strike. Tanzania was much the same.

These halls of learning were somewhat reminiscent of my tumultuous days at the University of North Carolina at Chapel Hill.

I grew up amidst sixteen sets of aunts and uncles and dozens of cousins, and no one had ever gone to college before me. My parents did not want me to attend that godless, communist school in Chapel Hill. They wanted me to go to a good church school like Duke or Davidson.

Needless to say, my family was politically conservative. My paternal grandmother always took a grandchild into the voting booth to show her where to mark the straight Republican ticket. My maternal grandparents fervently supported the Republican

Sheriff of Davie County, even after he lost his license due to multiple DUIs and had to be driven around.

When I tried to register to vote as a Democrat, the clerk said sternly, "I have to go get Mrs. Craver," who ran the Davidson County Board of Elections. She said, "Son, does your daddy know you are doing this? No one in your family has ever registered as a Democrat."

My parents changed their tune about Carolina when the Morehead Scholarship came my way. In one of those coincidences that changes your life, I will always be glad the letter from Duke awarding me the Angier B. Duke Scholarship did not arrive until a week later, saving me from that unimaginable fate.

I went to Carolina convinced I had gotten the Morehead by mistake and that they were going to take it back. This fear was reinforced on the first day of my English Honors class when we were told to read the entire *Odyssey* before the next class. A preppie next to me nonchalantly asked, "In English or Greek?"

My paranoia that my scholarship was in error was heightened midway through the semester, when one night all of my Morehead buddies started pulling out their tuxes in preparation for a freshman banquet I knew nothing about. Although I rarely left the library up to that point, I now doubled down in my studies, worried I would be discovered as an imposter. I found out years later what happened that night, and why I knew nothing of the formal affair. The J in my name stands for my first name, Jerry, which I never use. It turns out there was another Jerry Leonard on campus — an impoverished law student. He received my invitation in error. And although he had no idea why he was invited, I assume he figured a free meal was a free meal, so he took my invitation and went.

VICTORY FOR THE UNIVERSITY PARTY

Spring of my freshman year I decided to get involved in campus politics. I ran for the student legislature from Morrison Dorm on the University Party ticket, and I won.

That decision had consequences. The fall of my sophomore year, Charlie Mercer, who was Vice President and thus Speaker of the student legislature, suddenly announced he was leaving Carolina at the end of the fall semester to participate in a prestigious intern program through North Carolina State. I ran against a popular senior to replace him. We tied, 25-25, giving Charlie the chance to pick his successor. Charlie picked me, but only after an endless oration in which he addressed most of his personal problems and many of the world's.

CAFETERIA WORKERS' STRIKE

That was the year of the cafeteria workers' strike. I had come to know some of the workers, because they were the only people on campus who seemed like the folks from home. The more we talked, the more I came to see things their way. I joined the picket lines and became part of a coordinating committee of students organizing support. I authored and introduced a resolution in support of the workers' position. As Speaker, I pushed it through the student legislature.

One morning, I was told UNC President Bill Friday wanted to see me immediately. I went to his office, and he told me that he was afraid Governor Bob Scott was about to do something rash. He wanted a student to talk to him to explain that everything was peaceful and under control. I said when, and he said right now. I drove to Raleigh. Governor Scott and I talked for the better part of an hour. I thought it went well. But that night, Governor Scott invoked the public insurrection provision of the North Carolina Constitution and declared martial law on campus. We awoke to several hundred armed National Guardsmen lining the sidewalks.

Next time I saw President Friday, he said, "That didn't go like I hoped."

I just shrugged.

The workers' strike gave me my first exposure to the power of law. On the first day of the strike, a majority of the black students on campus went through Lenoir Hall turning over all of the chairs and tables to make it clear the dining hall was closed. The racist history professor who chaired the Faculty Committee on Scholarships decided he knew how to put an end to this. He immediately started proceedings to revoke the scholarships of all the participating students, on grounds of character and fitness.

The hearings were private, but that was when the University was experimenting with putting students on faculty committees. I was the student on that committee and could not be excluded from the hearings.

I was horrified. Not knowing what else to do, I went to the law school and asked to see Associate Dean Bob Byrd, whom I had met once before at a reception. I told him I knew much worse things happened in frat houses every Saturday night than what these students did in Lenoir Hall, and no one was taking away the frat brothers' scholarships. He noncommittally said he would look into it. The next morning, when the hearings resumed, Dean Byrd was there. He asked to speak to the chairman in the hall. A few minutes later, the chairman returned red-faced and announced the hearings were suspended indefinitely.

That was that.

Incidentally, the chairman got his revenge. He was also the advisor to Phi Beta Kappa. Then, the tradition was that the student with the highest GPA in your junior year was to be president. My year, three of us were tied, and he gleefully informed me he tossed a coin twice in the privacy of his office, and I had lost each time. I could be Secretary.

IN THE ORBIT OF THE QUEEN

My sophomore year I moved into the orbit of the legendary Anne Queen, the director of the Campus Y and the conscience of the University. I became a regular houseboy at her famous Saturday night cocktail parties.

There I met folks like Tom Lambert, Martha McKay, Howard Lee, John Sanders, and critically, Joel Fleishman.

Anne said to him, "This boy needs to go to Yale Law, and you need to make it happen."

Late one Saturday night, I watched President Friday and Senator Ralph Scott, the Governor's uncle, settle the workers' strike sitting on her sofa.

Although I pledged at Delta Upsilon fraternity and made lifelong friends there, a group of us began lobbying that spring for permission to form a coed living and academic space. Because the University thought no one would participate if they gave us the top two floors of James Dorm, we got permission to use those floors.

Thus was born the legendary Project Hinton. An exceptional group of coed students moved in there together, with our own dining hall, faculty fellows, and courses we designed.

VIETNAM WAR AND STOKELY CARMICHAEL

After the turmoil of the workers' strike my sophomore year, I returned to campus my junior year expecting quieter things. But then President Nixon, rather than ending the Vietnam War as promised, bombed Cambodia. Campuses across the country exploded.

I went with Wib Gulley, a Duke student, to the airport to pick up Jack Newfield, the legendary Village Voice columnist who was speaking at protest rallies on both campuses. The lead story the next week in the Village Voice went something like this, "If tall blond boys with thick drawls from Little Rock and Welcome are leading the protests, this war is almost over."

In the spring of my junior year, I didn't do what everyone expected. My friend Tom Bello and I agreed he would run for study body president and I would try for president of the Carolina Union. Although the student body president had the bully pulpit, the Union president had an enormous budget and control of concerts, movies, speakers, and events.

In most ways, my year as President of the Carolina Student Union was wonderful. I got to hang out with and introduce musical artists like Chicago, Ike and Tina Turner, Richie Havens, and John Sebastian. The great W.H. Auden agreed to a poetry reading, and I was able to bring my high school English teacher, a major reason for all of my academic success, to Chapel Hill for dinner with her idol.

Not that there wasn't the occasional hitch.

I agreed with the Black Student Movement that the Union would pay for a speaker of their choosing. They chose Stokely Carmichael, and so I invited him. A furious Chancellor summoned me to South Building and told me to withdraw the invitation.

I declined, saying, "I know you can overrule me, but do you really want us marching around again this year?"

Stokely Carmichael came and made an uneventful speech.

TELL IT TO THE ALLMAN BROTHERS

For all of its successes, my days at Carolina ended in ignominy: I am the guy who killed Jubilee.

In many ways, what happened nationally in the transition from Woodstock to Altamont happened locally on our campus. Before I got there, Jubilees were light-hearted spring festivals attended only by students and their dates. My year, folks began bringing us fliers from head shops up and down the East Coast.

"Come to Jubilee," said the flyers, with directions for getting there.

As a result, folks from all over the country descended on Chapel Hill for Jubilee. Mobs crashed and broke down the gates. None of our security systems worked. The straw bales used as seating for the bluegrass stage were set ablaze. Dozens of people were treated at the first aid tent for drug overdoses.

Again I witnessed the awesome power of the law, as neighbors obtained a temporary restraining order for Carolina Union director Howard Henry and me to be arrested if the music was not over by twelve. Try telling that to the Allman Brothers.

In truth, I was mostly relieved no one died.

It was on my watch that I advised Union Director Howard

Henry to end Jubilee forever. If not, it would be worse next year. I met with the Chancellor over the issue. A brief joint statement was released saying Jubilee was history.

Meanwhile, I slunk out of Chapel Hill.

Chapter 15

—

Barefoot and Happy in Tanzania

"You will find me here."
— Typical response of an African judge to
a request for a meeting

As my time in Tanzania came to a logical end, the Chief Justice and Mrs. Nyalali invited me to dinner at their official residence.

I was honored. It is uncommon for African officials to invite Americans into their homes. They usually prefer to entertain at restaurants or clubs. After a lovely meal, Mrs. Nyalali excused herself and the Chief Justice and I talked late into the evening over a bottle of Konyagi.

I finally said I must go, because I was keeping my driver away from his family. The Chief Justice said, "Send him away. We have more to discuss."

When I looked confused about how I would then return to my residence, he smiled and said, "Rich, I have drivers."

NATURAL BEAUTY

Native arts and crafts have a huge appeal for me, and I took advantage of my time in Africa to obtain some beautiful pieces. Our home is full of cranes and elephants from master carvers in Lusaka. Our beach house is adorned with a wall of colorful masks from the Luangwa River Valley and another wall of folk art from Ghana. Woven wool rugs from Namibia are spread about.

My absolute favorites, though, are the Tinga Tinga paintings of Tanzania, a unique style of one-dimensional, incredibly vibrant, almost cartoonish depictions of animals and scenes. I had bought many on prior trips. This time, I was looking for just the right one as a special present. I had yet to find it.

One day I took off for my customary jog. It was the day before I was to leave Tanzania, and I happened to run by the center where the Tinga Tinga painters worked. I spotted a lovely painting of an African scene. It was the perfect gift I had been looking for. Only one problem: I was jogging and had no money with me.

Undeterred, the painter looked me over and said, "I take your shoes."

I took off my Nikes and handed them to him. He gave me the painting, and I ran back to the hotel.

Barefoot and happy.

GENESIS OF **PACER** SYSTEM

The painting was for the chambers of my good friend Judge Ann Williams of Chicago, to whom I owed an enormous debt. Some background here is necessary.

The federal courts in the United States are truly a self-governing third branch. Our Congress is called the Judicial Conference of the United States, consisting of two judges from each of twelve circuits with the Chief Justice as chair. Like the Congress, it works through committees. Perhaps the most powerful is the Judicial Conference Committee on Court Administration and Case Management, known as CACM.

CACM consists of fourteen judges appointed by the Chief Justice, one from each of twelve circuits and a bankruptcy judge and magistrate judge. The chair normally names a federal clerk of court to work as an advisor to the committee. When I was a clerk, I was that person.

Judge Williams was on the CACM committee and we became fast friends.

In 1992, I became a federal bankruptcy judge. Shortly thereafter, Chief Justice William Rehnquist named Judge Williams as chair of CACM. When the bankruptcy judge seat on the committee came open, she went directly to the Chief Justice and successfully lobbied for my appointment, although there were many judges senior to me who thought it was their turn.

Prior to my first meeting in December of 1996, Judge Williams designated Judge John Lungstrum of Kansas and me as the two "executive sponsors" of the development of the new electronic filing and case management system to which the federal courts were transitioning, known as CM/ECF. In that capacity, we were told to meet with the godfather of automation in the federal courts, Judge Owen Forrester of Atlanta. For years, Judge Forrester had been the major voice pushing the federal courts in this direction, but his term was ending. As directed, we appeared at the restaurant of The Willard Hotel for the meeting. Judge

Forrester, a big man with a booming voice, sat in the back at a table alone, chain smoking. With no preliminaries, he explained that he was handing us the torch for the most important transition ever undertaken by the federal courts. He described in detail how the changes would revolutionize federal practice. He warned us not to mess it up and the meeting was over, with no food or drink for us. As we walked out, John turned to me and said, "What the fuck was that about?" We were soon to find out.

Being on the Judicial Conference Committee on Court Administration and Case Management put me in the middle of the major events happening in the federal courts. We were moving from an entirely paper to an entirely electronic case management system. I remember being at the table when we discussed whether anyone would be interested in dialing into our new database with a modem to retrieve information. That was the genesis of the world-famous PACER system, which makes federal cases virtually transparent to anyone with an internet connection.

Through CACM I became friends with remarkable judges.

I worked with the regal Susan Black of Florida to develop CHASER, the first tool for chambers access to the new system. When our colleagues complained that it was not sufficiently sophisticated, she quieted them: "I have built you a perfectly serviceable Ford. Drive it. We will get a Mercedes later."

John Koeltl of New York and I worked together to draft the first sets of model local rules to implement the new electronic filing and case management systems – John did the district courts and I took the bankruptcy courts.

But with transparency came concerns about infringement on litigants' privacy. Some of the bankruptcy courts, impatient with the slow pace of the federal transition to an electronic file, had begun to scan in all of their documents and make them publicly available on the Internet. When CACM met in Wyoming in the summer of 1997, I showed the Committee what was available on the local bankruptcy court's website. Bankruptcy petitions are a complete disclosure of the personal and financial lives of debtors, including social security and bank account numbers, minor children's names, and a plethora of other private information. The judges were horrified. One stated that she was looking to write the great American novel, and there was so much information in the bankruptcy file of one particular family that she had found her story. This immediately led to a six-judge task force appointed to come up with the first privacy rules.

When CSPAN decided to broadcast the public hearings of our Privacy Committee in spring 2001, I had to cut short a honeymoon trip to Portugal with my wife Whitney in order to attend.

The privacy issues our task force grappled with were not easy ones. Our Chairman was my great buddy John Lungstrum of Kansas, who by then had replaced Judge Williams as Chair of CACM. John and I were usually in agreement, but on one particular issue we differed: John thought there should be a delay period after documents were filed before public access was provided, so that intrusions into personal privacy could be detected and prevented.

I vehemently disagreed. I thought that if the public record wasn't synchronous with the actual filings, the result would be deceptive and unreliable. My equally good buddy, Sam Wilson of Virginia, saw it my way. The rest of the committee began to agree with us also. John, as chair, refused to yield. He kept the discussion going.

Sam got up to leave the room, and John remarked, "This is a heck of a time to walk out."

"I have the votes," Sam replied sharply. "I can pee when I want."

We worked it out, and our basic principles are now codified in all of the federal rules of procedure.

FOCUS, GLADYS, FOCUS

Long days of intense discussion of hard issues during CACM meetings morphed into boisterous games of Trivial Pursuit by night. Judges, spouses, and guests would divide into two teams, largely by gender. My wife would coordinate the women's team, I would lead the men. Never were so many powerful egos, of judges and equally brilliant guests, in play.

One of our favorite participants was the legendary Gladys Kessler, the district judge from D.C. who had presided over so many critical cases of national import. Judge Kessler was an oral processor, and she would often try out an answer by saying the first thing that came to mind. This was not a successful strategy for a team event. After two or three missteps, my professor-wife took matters under control. She put her hands on Judge Kessler's shoulders, looked her square in the eye, and said, "Gladys, I need you to slow down, and I need you to focus." The group collectively held its breath until Judge Kessler chortled and said, "I love you, Whitney." My buddy John Lungstrum whispered to me, "I know lawyers who would pay a lot of money to say that."

"Focus, Gladys, focus" became the good-natured mantra for our group.

A painting for Judge Williams was the least I could do to pay her back for these opportunities.

Fresh From the Bush

At times during these years, I felt like my life was on the verge of spiraling out of control. It seemed as if I had four full-time jobs: the bankruptcy docket, the work in Africa, involvement in national judicial administration, and serving as Editor-in-Chief of the American Bankruptcy Law Journal.

The only reason all these plates kept spinning was because of the skill and calm of my judicial assistant, Cathy Barnes.

Cathy could simultaneously master my Africa travel schedule, organize a meeting of a national task force, and proofread and cite-check every court opinion and law review article to make sure her standard of zero tolerance for mistakes was met. One afternoon, when I sharply asked why she had cleared my calendar for the rest of the day, she retorted, "It's your wife's fortieth birthday. You might need to pay attention."

On my last night in Dar, the judges and court officials with whom I had worked for several years took me out for an evening of eating, drinking, and dancing. After the meal, a large wooden box appeared on the dance floor. The dancers circled the box, everyone beating on it. Suddenly, the lid was removed, and a 15-foot python lunged straight for me. I backed up so suddenly I broke the legs off of my chair, to the great amusement of my friends. This snake was "fresh from the bush, caught that day." So lively.

I don't like snakes, but rather than humiliate my country further, I moved to the floor for the required ceremonial dance with the snake. We stretched it out among several of us, preventing it from wrapping around anyone.

Part 3
Namibia

—

"His way had therefore come full circle,
or rather had taken the form of an ellipse
or a spiral, following as ever
no straight unbroken line."

Hermann Hesse

Chapter 16

—

Namibia and Working ATMs

"Learning expands great souls."
— Namibian proverb

Arriving in Namibia one Sunday afternoon, I saw everywhere huge renditions of the number "10." The country had just celebrated its tenth birthday as an independent nation.

Namibia has a tortured history. It was awarded to Germany in the great carve-up of Africa by European sovereigns in the late nineteenth century.

When Germany lost World War I, it was stripped of all its colonies. Then known as German South West Africa, it became a protectorate under the League of Nations. So far, so good, except that the League turned it over to South Africa. This continued after World War II; although the United Nations established direct supervision of the colony, South Africa disputed its legitimacy to do so and remained in complete control.

South Africa did nothing for the native Namibians, instead treating the colony as just another province. All of their brutal apartheid policies applied. Years of revolutionary struggle, with the rebels increasingly backed by most of the world, finally led to success in 1990. Interestingly, in their 1990 constitution, the Namibians made English the official language of government, even though only ten percent of the populace spoke it at that time. The Namibians were having nothing to do with the more commonly spoken German and Afrikaans, the languages of their oppressors. Namibia has three primary tribes of roughly equal influence who speak three different languages, so picking one of those was inappropriate. English was what was left, and so won by default.

In Namibia, as in every other country I visited, everyone is at least bilingual. Most speak three or four languages. Africans speak the dialect of their tribe and usually that of adjacent tribes, and are conversant in the dominant national languages, whether they be English, German, Afrikaans, or French. During one road trip, I watched a friend converse fluently with us in English, then talk on the phone to her family in German, to her University colleagues in Afrikaans, and to the workers on her farm in Herero.

Because most Africans are exposed to different languages at an early age, they pick up new languages quickly.

I stayed one weekend at a new desert lodge in the Namib Desert and the manager told me a story. She said when the lodge opened, she had a great deal of difficulty communicating with the local staff. After a couple of months of floundering in their native dialect, they asked for a meeting. They politely informed her, "Madam, from now on speak to us in Afrikaans. Now we all know it."

Namibia was different from other African countries where I consulted. Basically, everything worked. The power grid was stable, the water system was safe, and the roads rivaled those in the United States in construction and maintenance.

Driving in my first morning, I noticed lines of people on every street corner. I asked my driver what was going on.

"In America you not have ATMs? Everyone spent their money during the weekend and are lined up to get more for the week."

As brutal as apartheid was, the South Africans were ruthlessly efficient when it came to building systems. Namibia was a different Africa than I had seen.

As in most of Africa, the study of law in Namibia is an undergraduate major. It takes five years to complete, and to become a legal practitioner you must be attached to a firm or another approved institution for a year and then pass a bar exam.

Africans choose law at a much earlier age, unlike the experience of most American students, who can literally use any undergraduate degree as a springboard to law.

Many students, like me, decide on law at the last moment.

Chapter 17

—

A Davidson County Boy in New Haven

"I have never let my schooling interfere with my education."
— Mark Twain

As I neared the end of college, I was drawn towards both law and educational administration. In North Carolina at that time, lawyers ran higher education. Bill Friday was president of the University of North Carolina system, Terry Sanford was president of Duke University, and Ferebee Taylor was Chancellor of the University of North Carolina at Chapel Hill.

I wavered between going to law school and getting a graduate degree in education.

Yale Law School held particular appeal, as it had a reputation for training its graduates for a broad range of professions with a less-traditional curriculum. I applied to Yale Law School, and also graduate school in education at UNC. Not surprisingly, I found myself on the waitlist for law school but admitted to graduate school, which I started in May.

A letter that arrived by special delivery less than two months later changed everything. The letter said I was admitted to Yale

Law but had to accept within 48 hours. I had just finished one session of summer school and started another, so I made the reasonable request to defer a year to finish my master's degree.

Yale was having none of it.

I was gently told I was the last one in, and unless I enrolled that fall, I was unlikely ever to see New Haven.

I pivoted my educational plans.

At Yale, no rooms were available in law school housing, and I had very little money. I found a one-bedroom efficiency apartment close to the law school. When I told my landlord I was looking for a place near the gym, he laughed and told me the massive building across the street I had mistaken for a cathedral was, in fact, the gym.

A few weeks later, my worried parents drove me to Connecticut to start school. They kept a game face but were concerned about where I would be living and the desolation of New Haven. I lived on the most dangerous street in the city. Returning to my apartment late at night from the library, I would pause at the corner of the gym and run the last block as fast as I could to keep from getting mugged.

My dad told me later that on the ride home after dropping me off at law school, my mother cried all the way to Maryland headed back to North Carolina.

AM I THE DUMBEST PERSON HERE?

The pressures of Yale Law were not mainly academic. If you did the work, you would be fine. Instead, the pressure emanated from the brilliance and sophistication of the faculty and your fellow students. For the first time in my life, I looked around a classroom and thought, "I could be the dumbest person here."

The faculty was luminary. James William Moore of Moore's Federal Practice, the leading authority on civil procedure in the nation, led off my first class in his last year of teaching. I started out with Robert Bork for constitutional law. When he left to become Solicitor General, I was switched to Alexander Bickel, who had to take time off mid-semester to prepare for and argue the Pentagon Papers case in the Supreme Court. The brilliant Guido Calabresi, later to be dean and a judge on the Second Circuit, taught torts. My personal nemesis was Ellen Peters for contracts. Later to be the Chief Justice of Connecticut, her withering Socratic interrogations gave me a persistent case of insomnia. I sat down the row from Clarence Thomas in constitutional law, and from his writings realized that he felt similarly.

The students were equally frightening. When I asked Lovida Coleman (later to become a good buddy) what she was doing the first weekend, she replied, "Going to Paris." She explained that her dad, who was later to become the Secretary of Transportation, was on the board of Pan Am. She had a card that let her fly free whenever there was an empty seat on a plane.

Others were headed down to Queens to sit in their family box for the opening weekend of the U.S. Open.

I was overwhelmed. I did not feel well after the second day of class and went to the brand new student infirmary, which had just opened that week. I told the doctor, "I am sure this is psychosomatic, as I am struggling to fit in here."

He laughed as he admitted me.

"You can't give yourself a fever of 103."

I was the first student to ever spend a night in that infirmary.

Two weeks into class, I had had enough. I decided to leave Yale and head back to North Carolina. I packed my bags to return home.

But being a polite Southerner, I stopped by to tell Dean Jim Thomas, the kind Dean of Students, I was leaving. Yale Law takes so few students that I thought, possibly, there was still time for someone to replace me. It was a conversation that changed the course of my life. He gently explained that mine was a common reaction, particularly for students who had come from more remote parts of the country. He urged me to gut out a semester. As per Yale's policy, if I successfully completed the first semester, I could re-enroll any time within five years, no questions asked. If I left now, I was done.

I went back to my dismal apartment and unpacked.

I did what Dean Thomas said, but never made peace with the place that first semester. When I went home for Christmas, I drove the family car back to New Haven, so that I could leave as soon as I was done with exams. I left law school, returned to Chapel Hill, and finished my master's degree in education.

Dropping out of law school gnawed at me. I had never failed at anything. Additionally, I wanted a higher degree, and the idea of suffering through a doctorate in education was stifling.

I wrote Yale and re-enrolled eighteen months later.

By then, my life had changed. I had coupled up with the woman who was to become my first wife. We went through undergraduate school and graduate school together, and she was by my side. We moved into a warm, congenial house on Derby Avenue with two friends from my first run, Dirk Shenkkan, who was to become a prominent San Francisco lawyer, and Charlie Brown, who would be the Attorney General of West Virginia. His little brother Sherrod, now a senator from Ohio, was a Yale undergraduate and was omnipresent at our house. I met my good friends from UNC, Tom and Judy Bello, on the docks in New York City with a rental truck as they disembarked from the Queen Elizabeth II. They were returning from Tom's Rhodes Scholarship in England, both to be classmates.

We became the center of a tight group of inseparable friends.

Every spring break, I rented a huge house on the North Carolina Outer Banks and brought the group south for their first time. Because we were desperately poor, I worked twenty hours a week at New Haven Legal Aid. Most of my clients were African Americans who emigrated from the Carolinas.

Anchoring it for me was a remarkable friendship with a wealthy Jewish guy from Queens, Steve Goode. No one could figure out why he and a poor North Carolina redneck were best buddies.

Neither could we, but we were.

Near the end of our time at Yale, Steve disappeared. I could not find him anywhere and suspected a romantic entanglement he could not even confess to me. He was, I learned, writing a law review note. You join the Yale Law Journal by writing a publishable note. Our anti-elitist group largely scoffed at the prospect, but Steve hoped for a career in academia and needed membership on the Journal to complete his resume. He figured if he joined at the end, his name would only be on the masthead once, and none of us would see it.

It worked. Steve wrote for the Journal and has had a long career on the faculty of the University of Texas School of Law.

A Law Degree and a Six-Month-Old Baby

The final time my parents drove up to New Haven was to see their son walk across the stage at graduation from Yale Law School, holding their six-month-old grandson. With a spectacular record herself, my wife was admitted to Yale Law after our first year in New Haven. Law school posed little difficulty to someone of her intellect, so she suggested we go ahead and use the time to start a family.

Women students in large numbers were a fairly recent addition at Yale. Students married to each other were a rarity, and a married couple with an infant was a novelty. The carrels in the law library are in rows of three seats. Our middle seat was stocked with diapers, wipes, toys, and a portable seat. In classic Yale Law School tradition, the administration, so afraid to make a mistake, went out of its way to accommodate us. Although my wife had a year to go, Yale allowed her to do that year at the University of North Carolina School of Law so that we could move home and I could start my clerkship.

Still maximizing her time, she was pregnant again that year. Our second son was born the summer after she finished. It worked. After three years of law school, four semesters of which she was pregnant, she had a law degree and two gorgeous little boys.

Onward and Upward

The career trajectories of my classmates have been extraordinary.

Although I crossed paths with Bill Clinton and Hillary Rodham during my unhappy first semester, they were gone by the time I returned. I did not know them, except possibly in a passing sense. A rigorous fitness class was held at 5 pm every day at the Yale gym. It was mandatory for off-season athletes, but anyone could attend. I rarely missed. I am pretty sure Hillary was also a regular, although I have never confirmed it with her.

Five of us – Clarence Thomas, Sam Alito, Willie Fletcher, Guy Cole, and I – were nominated to the federal courts of appeals around the country in the 1990s. The other four made it and have had distinguished careers, with Clarence and Sam moving on to be Justices of the U.S. Supreme Court.

But Jesse Helms was my senior senator, so I remained a trial judge with the federal bankruptcy court.

Chapter 18

—

On to Windhoek

"Little by little, a little becomes a lot."
— African proverb

Out of the window of my hotel in Windhoek, Namibia, on a hill across the street, I could see a stunning building. Made of pink marble, it undulated across the hillside to mimic the famous Namibian dunes. The hotel manager told me, "Oh, that is our new Supreme Court. The Chinese built it for us." That was my first exposure to the brazen Chinese strategy to insinuate its presence into virtually every African nation.

My tour in Namibia began by meeting with their gracious Chief Justice, Johan Strydom. Unlike in the other countries I visited, white Africans like Chief Justice Strydom sat on the Namibian courts. During the revolutionary struggle, Strydom was a fearless advocate defending the rebel leaders when they were incarcerated, and later a sympathetic High Court judge. He was rewarded with an appointment to Chief Justice.

A cheerful man with a quick wit, he took his job with utmost seriousness.

"I am the John Marshall of Namibia," he told me. "Everything I write about our new constitution is the first word."

ADR AND A NEW MARRIAGE

My work in Namibia was different than what I had done in Zambia and elsewhere in Africa. The courts in Namibia were nicely organized with precise record-keeping and meticulous file rooms. Improving case management wasn't the primary concern. Instead, court officials were struggling to deal with a huge backlog and growing caseload.

The Chief Justice heard about alternative dispute resolution (ADR) and was interested in exploring it. We decided he would appoint a formal commission, known as the Commission on the Reduction of Costs and Delay, and I and other experts would provide the staffing.

I knew just where to turn.

A senior researcher at the Federal Judicial Center was Donna Stienstra, who also happened to be one of the top authorities on setting up ADR programs. She had written on the topic extensively and worked with numerous courts in the United States and abroad to set up their programs. She was also an inveterate traveler, having joined me on a trip to Zambia. She jumped at the chance to return to Namibia with me.

My personal life had also taken a happy turn. I remarried in 2000, to a fabulous young psychology professor at Peace College, halfway between my house and my courthouse. Our twentieth anniversary was in 2020, and I still feel like a newlywed. An adventurous soul, too, my wife was eager to come with me to Namibia.

By this time, I had become close friends with Gerhard Maritz, a judge of remarkable talent. Another white African, Gerhard had previously been the highest compensated litigator in the country. Completely happy in his lucrative practice, he told me the President summoned him and said he was being appointed to the High Court. When he protested, the President informed him that if he believed in his new country, it was his duty.

"The white business community must have confidence in our courts, and you sitting there will give them that confidence," said the President.

Gerhard and his lovely wife, Connie, also a college professor, lived in a strikingly modern home that Gerhard designed in the hills above Windhoek, the capital and largest city in Namibia.

When I told him Whitney was coming to Namibia with me, and that we had scheduled a vacation week before my work started, he had a ready answer. He said some of his close friends owned a tourist camp on the Namibia and Botswana border in the far north of the country. But it was also close to Angola, where some French tourists had been murdered in a highway assault several weeks earlier. This was mildly troubling. In fact, the entire area had been declared a "no travel" zone.

Nonetheless, Gerhard said he could make the arrangements, and he was certain it was safe. But he said there was one condition: Under no circumstances could any of the American diplomats know we had gone there. Both Whitney and I happily agreed.

THE VACATION OF A LIFETIME

We landed in Windhoek, immediately climbed into the four-seater plane waiting on us, and in a couple of hours landed on the dirt strip at Gerhard's friends' lodge.

It was the vacation of a lifetime. We were the only guests. The staff was bored beyond measure and created adventure after adventure for us.

We took long game drives and tailed herds of elephants. Every afternoon we took a boat cruise. The staff would stop the boat at a different spot each afternoon, disembark, and set up a table for snacks and "sundowners," the local cocktail. We had a private cabin away from the lodge and awoke to the sounds of monkeys on our roof and hippos heading back into the river after a night of grazing on shore. A 12-foot-long crocodile, named "Nandie" by the staff, responded remarkably to my wife's voice. Each morning Whitney would call her, and we would see the reeds rustle along the riverbank. Nandie would then appear at the dock for her morning snack.

As our week ended, we sat beside the dirt landing strip as the plane to take us to Windhoek appeared, dipped its wing, and reversed course without landing. They radioed that they had a bad battery, and that once turned off the engine could not restart.

I called Gerhard, who was furious. He immediately called the President of Namibia Air, who sent his private plane to pick us up.

DON'T UPSET THE OSTRICH

The next weekend, Gerhard and Connie hosted us at their farm a couple of hours north of Windhoek. Namibia is largely a desert, so farms are vast in order to have enough grazing land for livestock. Gerhard had a fleet of four-wheelers to cover his property, and he insisted that we each take one and go for a tour.

My wife, a bit of a girly-girl, wasn't enthused, but went along anyway. All was well until we apparently got too close to a nest. A massive female ostrich singled out my wife as the culprit and attacked. Gerhard saved the day with a circling move that cut off the mother bird just before she assaulted my wife.

"Next time I tell you I don't want to do something, please listen," she muttered under her breath.

Whitney shared my enchantment with Namibia, to the point that she looked into the possibility of returning there to teach for a semester. She scheduled an hour-long appointment with the psychology faculty at the University of Namibia. At the end of that hour, the driver returned without her.

"Still they talk," he said.

He returned an hour later, alone, frustrated, and perplexed.

"And still they talk." On his third try, he returned her to the hotel.

COMMISSION ON THE REDUCTION OF COSTS AND DELAY

The work Donna and I did in Namibia was substantive and efficient. The Commission on the Reduction of Costs and Delay appointed by the Chief Justice consisted of thoughtful judges and lawyers who grappled with the material we brought them. We laid out the basic principles of ADR, primarily mediation, and empirically demonstrated the enormous impact it had in other legal systems.

Even so, it took some persuading for them to buy in.

The Namibian courts, like those throughout Africa, were hierarchical, formal, and autocratic. Mediation is a much more informal process, with fluid give-and-take and fewer fixed rules.

For instance, the concept that statements made during mediation can never be used in formal litigation was hard for the group to swallow. In their view, an admission against interest should always be able to be used in court. In the end they came around to seeing the merits of ADR, and Namibia now has a mandatory mediation program for civil cases in the High Court.

FRIENDS AT PLAY

On what I thought would be my last trip there, two of my closest friends, Thomas Sayre and Gray Medlin, joined me for a week of play. Thomas and I crossed paths at Carolina as students. In fact, I was his orientation counselor. We had lost track until we met at a seminar at UNC in 1990, and he told me he and his family had relocated to downtown Raleigh.

We began meeting weekly to design art, deconstruct lawsuits, and drink Monday night martinis. Thomas was a partner in an architecture firm but was beginning to make a name for himself as a world-renowned sculptor.

One of my proudest accomplishments is having design credit on a sculpture Thomas made. It graces the entrance to the courthouse in Clearwater, Florida. I drew it on a napkin one Monday night.

In return, Thomas – who in addition to being a brilliant artist is also wickedly smart – helped me untangle any number of hopelessly complex lawsuits.

When my first marriage ended in the summer of 1994, one of the saddest consequences for me was losing our house on Lake

Gaston. My wife and I had amicably agreed it would go to her, in exchange for my keeping our house in town. We bought the lake house when our boys were three and two, and fond childhood memories are tied to the place. I spent many weekends there with a tribe of little boys.

Thomas and his lovely wife, Joan Ellen Deck (known to all as Jed), came to my rescue. They and their two little girls were also looking for a lake house getaway to escape the downtown Raleigh summer heat. They suggested we join forces and buy one together. We found a funky old house on a couple of acres jutting out into the lake. It has been a wonderful partnership for decades. I did all of the legal work and paid the bills, and Thomas drew the plans and oversaw the renovation. Jed and I did the landscaping, until we finally just surrendered to the deer who ate everything.

At the time, I was in the process of being nominated to the Fourth Circuit. In those more innocent days, I really thought it would happen. If it had, I would have spent the rest of my professional days commuting between Raleigh and the court headquarters in Richmond. A lake house halfway between would be a real asset. That was not to be, of course. But as Thomas and Jed's daughters grew up and moved on, it was there for me to introduce another set of young Leonards to the joys of laidback leisure time at the lake.

Thomas and I would frequently slip away, just the two of us, for long hikes over the abandoned rail lines, lengthy bike rides, and other adventures. Often we would go to the lake after dark and swim for an hour or more. One night, as we were in the water and turned to go home, a surprisingly strong current made the going difficult.

Thomas said, "Let's just go knock on a neighbor's door and ask for a ride."

"That won't work," I replied. "You forgot we are skinny dipping."

On we stroked until we made it safely back home.

A RETURN TO RAINIER

Gray Medlin and I met in 1994, when our wives took their leave at almost the same time. We were wounded and embarrassed but found solace in each other's company. Every Thursday night we met at his house to watch Grey's Anatomy. We took our running to a new level, training for a marathon and crossing the finish line together just under our four-hour goal. We flew to Miami, rented a white Mustang, and played in the Keys for a few days.

After our Kilimanjaro climb, John Edwards and I still had a reservation to summit Mount Rainier the next summer. But when the time came, John was uninterested in going, so Gray took his place.

For the second time I climbed Mount Rainier. This was a much easier trip, ascending under a moonlit sky instead of a blizzard.

Peculiarly, the climbing company had a policy of not allowing friends to climb together on the same rope line. In its experience, friends pushed each other past exhaustion and into a danger zone. So I did not see Gray until the summit, where, instead of his usual smile, I was greeted with a grimace.

"I fell and really hurt my knee," he said.

He descended leaning on a guide and using his ice axe as a crutch.

Once off the mountain, we went immediately to a hospital in

Seattle, where doctors treated a bad bruise. We continued on the trip as planned, exploring Seattle and Victoria. Gray was on crutches, in obvious pain when the Percocet wore off. I became a little impatient at why a bruise was so messing with our trip.

Back home in Raleigh, Gray visited his orthopedist. His kneecap was cracked in three places, but the cracks were only visible when x-rayed from behind. The hospital in Seattle had completely missed it. His doctor said it was a miracle his kneecap did not completely disintegrate as he was descending Rainier.

I apologized to him.

BIBLICAL SCENE IN ETOSHA

When Thomas and Gray arrived in Namibia, we rented a car and headed immediately for one of the great game viewing areas in Africa, Etosha National Park in northern Namibia.

Namibia is largely a desert, particularly in August, the driest month of the year. Etosha is organized around about forty water holes in a vast area, and the animals are forced to those holes.

Tourists get a map and are allowed free access to roam, so long as you stay in your cars. Elephants, giraffes, cheetahs, buffalo, impala, kudos, monkeys, and lions drank in waves. The scene was Biblical in scope.

We sat entranced for two days.

Chapter 19

—

It's All About People

"Let a thousand fall before Africa be given up."
— Rev. Melville B. Cox, minister at Edenton Street Methodist
Church in Raleigh and first American Methodist Missionary
to Africa, who died weeks after arriving there in 1833.

One of the many fond memories from my time in Windhoek with my friends Thomas and Gray was finding a gym that provided the best workout we ever had. It was circuit training with thirty stops, governed by a stoplight that set green light intervals of thirty seconds. At the end, we were on the ground, panting and exhausted. We could not wait to return the next day to do it again.

Daily workouts have always been a part of my life. As a boy growing up in Welcome, I carefully measured to find the telephone pole that was exactly one mile down the road from our house, so I knew where to turn around on my nightly two-mile run. I made a set of weights out of tobacco sticks and firewood I clandestinely kept in the barn loft. In college and law school, I played endless games of pickup basketball, often resulting in a stint on crutches. I liked to play as if I was taller than my actual six feet, one inch height.

The intramural championship game at Yale was between teams from the law school and medical school. Always a brutal event, it was a harbinger of the antipathy to come.

My sons found soccer, and I started coaching their teams. I grew obsessed with the game and joined the adult league. It was the favorite part of my week for years, until an injury intervened. My teammate who played midfield alongside me said, "Lay down. I'm a doctor. I just heard your ACL pop."

"I hope you're right," I said. "I'm a lawyer."

EXERCISING BODY AND MIND

My steady workout partner for more than two decades has been Paul Ridgeway. We met as often as we could, but always late on Friday afternoon to lift weights. One Christmas, my wife, herself a fitness fan and certified Pilates instructor, decided I needed to pick up my game. She hired a trainer but knew I was unlikely to go alone. She included Paul in the gift. Devon the Divine, as we came to call him, worked out of a decrepit gym, a throwback to the 1950s. Where the serious bodybuilders in town hung out.

My fearless wife worked out there alone, with the same trainer. One of our favorites was a former professional football player she called Tiny. He endeared himself to me one morning by refusing to do the sit ups his trainer wanted.

"My abs are like the Lost Colony," he said. "They have been gone a long time, nobody knows where they went, and there's no use to go looking for them."

I thought his nickname was actually Tiny, and so greeted him regularly as such. He was polite but chilly, and soon I understood why. I overheard him say to a friend, "My name is Richard. If that cracker judge calls me Tiny one more time I am going to take him down." My wife thought it hysterical.

Devon pushed us to the limit, and we lifted more weight than we ever thought possible. One afternoon, Paul said, "Go into the locker room and tell me what's going on." A naked guy was standing on a plastic sheet while another guy, similarly attired, used a paint brush to cover him with tanning solution. They were preparing for a competition. "I think I'm done here," said Paul.

WE RETURNED TO THE Y.

A bit of competition underlies my friendship with Paul. One afternoon, he was having shoulder trouble. Although I was supposed to be spotting him, the weight was light and I wasn't paying attention. He dropped it on his chest, and I laughed.

A couple of weeks later, we were scheduled to go to New Bern to ride in the weekend MS 150 bike ride, 75 miles each day. Paul is a better biker than me, and I was mystified when he pulled us away from the main group onto a separate route. An optional century ride allowed you to go 100 miles a day. At about 85 miles, I was spent.

"Paul, you've got to slow down and pull me or I'm not going to make it," I said. He looked back over his shoulder.

"You shouldn't have laughed."

Our schedule became more difficult as Paul moved onto the superior court and then became the judge in charge as the senior resident. I moved to Campbell Law School as Dean. But we adjusted, and now, joined by Thomas Sayre, swim together at dawn three mornings a week, with coffee after. There, we solve the world's problems.

MORE FAMILY, LESS AFRICA

My life changed again with the birth of our first daughter, Louise Gray, in 2004, followed by her sister, Libba, in 2006, and her brother, Cain, in 2008. I returned to Africa twice for short trips after Louise Gray was born. By that point, I had obtained a seat on the Africa Council of the American Bar Association, and I flew to Kenya to represent the American Bar Association at an international conference on human trafficking.

Shortly after, I accepted an invitation to do a case management workshop for Nigerian High Court judges in Abuja. That was my hardest crowd. If I did not say something funny or provocative each and every minute, my audience got distracted, turning to each other and their cell phones.

As our family grew, I lost interest in being away from them for extended periods. It seemed risky to be so far removed, and the load on my working spouse left behind would have been considerable.

Plus the invitations were not coming as in the past. It is the nature of this work that if you're not visible, you're not remembered.

But my consulting days weren't quite over. In 2014, Chief Justice John Robert's Chief of Staff called and told me the new Namibian Chief Justice, Peter Shivute, had just visited D.C. I knew Peter from years earlier, when he was the newest and shyest High Court judge. The Namibians had adopted a new constitutional provision, which shifted control of the courts from the minister of justice to the chief justice, and he had asked if I could return to help in structuring the new judicial system.

I was elated. The model throughout Africa was similar, and the professed independence of the courts was ethereal, as the executive was able to exert indirect control over their activities through his minister. In every country I worked, I politely suggested that progress would be hard without removing this structural difficulty. The Namibians were the only ones who took it to heart.

There was even better news. Because I was no longer a government employee (I left my judgeship to become Dean of Campbell Law School in 2013), and the flight was more than eight hours, I could fly business class. I was thrilled. For two decades I had been crammed into coach seats for interminable flights, as our government won't pay for anything else for employees on official business.

Seating on these long flights was a guerilla war. As soon as the doors closed, folks began jockeying for position to find an extra seat or two, to stretch out to sleep. If lucky, you could find an entire unoccupied row in the rear. On one jammed flight, another big guy and I actually had an empty middle seat between us in a row of three. We breathed a sigh of relief as the doors closed, only to reopen momentarily for a late arrival. Down the aisle, heading toward us, was a huge Texan, our middle-seat companion. Nervous, he said, "I was named employee of the year by my company, and my prize was a hunting trip. I just wanted to go up in the hills and shoot deer. I had no idea they were sending me to Africa."

FRIED CRUNCHY WORMS

Sometimes, the planes did not take off at all. One evening, on a fully loaded 747 leaving Johannesburg, we were delayed in departing. Maintenance men came and went. Then, bizarrely, they brought out the dinner service and fed us at the gate. Someone, it turns out, flushed a dirty blanket down the toilet and completely jammed the plane's plumbing. The airline knew we would not leave that evening, but also that there was no place in the airport or hotel to eat dinner so late. We left the next morning.

Unwilling to break up a successful team, I had asked if my friend Donna Stienstra could again accompany me to Namibia. The first person I saw at the court was the former Chief Justice, Johan Strydom, who was sitting specially as a retired justice. He looked up as if I had just left the day before.

"Well, hello, Rich," he boomed. "You told us to do this ten years ago, and we finally got around to it."

Donna and I spent a delightful two weeks in Windhoek, talking with Chief Justice Shivute, justices and judges, the Minister of Justice, court administrators, and lawyers about the shape the new administrative structure should take. We left them a blueprint that was largely adopted by the Namibian Parliament shortly thereafter. We celebrated on our last night in Windhoek with an elegant dinner in our favorite restaurant overlooking the city, enjoying what had come to be our favorite appetizer of crunchy fried worms.

Chapter 20

—

The Journey Comes Full Circle

"The end of all our exploring will be to arrive where we started and know the place for the first time."
— T. S. Eliot

My love affair with Africa continues unabated.

I am never sure of the importance of the work I did there. My early goals to save the continent morphed later into a more sophisticated view to do no harm. I do know, however, that for me it was completely transformative. When I talk to other Africaphiles, we often have trouble putting into words the extraordinary draw the continent has on us.

It may be that, at some deeply subconscious level, we realize we have come home to the origin of our species, where we first stood upright and became fully human.

But there was another, more specific, attraction for me.

In Africa, family and clan are everything. Identity is defined by your people and comes with a host of responsibilities and obligations to those of your blood. This was also how I was raised. My father was the twelfth of fifteen children, my mother the second of four. I grew up with 16 sets of aunts and uncles and lived next door to my paternal grandparents, where my dad was born. My playmates were my 40 first cousins.

Our social life revolved entirely around family. We left church every Sunday and drove 25 miles to my maternal grandparents' house for lunch with my mother's entire clan. Mid-afternoon, we returned home to gather with my father's even larger clan in the front yard of the farmhouse. There were enough cousins to play softball in the barn yard, full teams of nine. Conversation focused entirely on the lives of various members of the family, with a healthy reverence for those who had gone before. About the time we became teenagers, we hired out as day laborers to aunts and uncles who raised tobacco or were truck farmers. I spent much of my summers working on my grandparents' dairy farm.

My grandparents were loving but tough. My maternal grand-mother adored me, her oldest grandchild, and I adored her. She once told me to hoe her row of beans to get the grass out. It was hot and buggy, so instead I lounged under the pear tree. Suddenly, I was lifted off the ground by my ear, and the voice of God said, "I'll have no grandson before I raise a sorry one."

It remains a powerful motivator. Years later, my grandmother was terminally ill the summer I took the bar exam. I drove from the final day of testing to her hospital room, where we spent her last night. The doctors told me she had kept herself alive by sheer will, muttering about "not messing up the big test."

My grandpa was the softer of the two. Visiting them on the farm some years earlier, before I was to leave for New Haven for law school, he suggested we go for a walk through the orchard. Something was on his mind.

"This Yale you're going to, is it thought to be a good school?"

I assured him it was. He continued, "I don't rightly get it. They always told me you were good with the books."

I assured him I had done fine. Puzzled, he continued. "So, you got to go a thousand miles to find a law school that will have you?" From the viewpoint of a man with a formal education ending in the second grade, it made little sense.

The similarity between my Southern upbringing and African culture goes even deeper. There are strong African traditions of sorcery and magic, and my paternal grandmother, who lived next door, was a "witching woman." She could make warts and boils disappear and "talk the fire out of a burn." Strangers were always screeching into the barnyard looking for help from Miss Nealie. I often saw her behind the smoke-house muttering incantations and burying stuff. The organization of African society is eerily similar to that of the rural South, of my childhood in Welcome.

Maybe that is why I have always felt at home there, in Africa.

My initial misgivings in 1994 that I was the wrong person were misplaced. I formed deep and lasting friendships with many people, across many cultures and countries. I know I participated in serious and meaningful work. I hope I provided a modicum of help. I believe I did no harm.

About the Author

—

Over the course of his long career, Rich Leonard has been a pioneering judge, a groundbreaking court administrator, a restorer of historic courthouses, and at age 29 the youngest U.S. District Court Clerk in the country, which gave him a front-row seat to some of the most sensational trials in North Carolina history.

He has also run marathons, climbed mountains, forged cross-continental friendships, and embraced life in all its majesty and messiness.

He worked as a special consultant to the U.S. Department of State, where for 20 years he helped developing countries in sub-Saharan Africa create workable court systems.

He is now the Dean of Campbell Law School in Raleigh, North Carolina, where he resides with his family.

CPSIA information can be obtained
at www.ICGtesting.com
Printed in the USA
LVHW081139050323
740957LV00023B/1556/J